# KNITTED
# MENAGERIE

# KNITTED
# MENAGERIE

## 30 ADORABLE CREATURES TO KNIT

Sarah Keen

THE GUILD OF MASTER CRAFTSMAN PUBLICATIONS

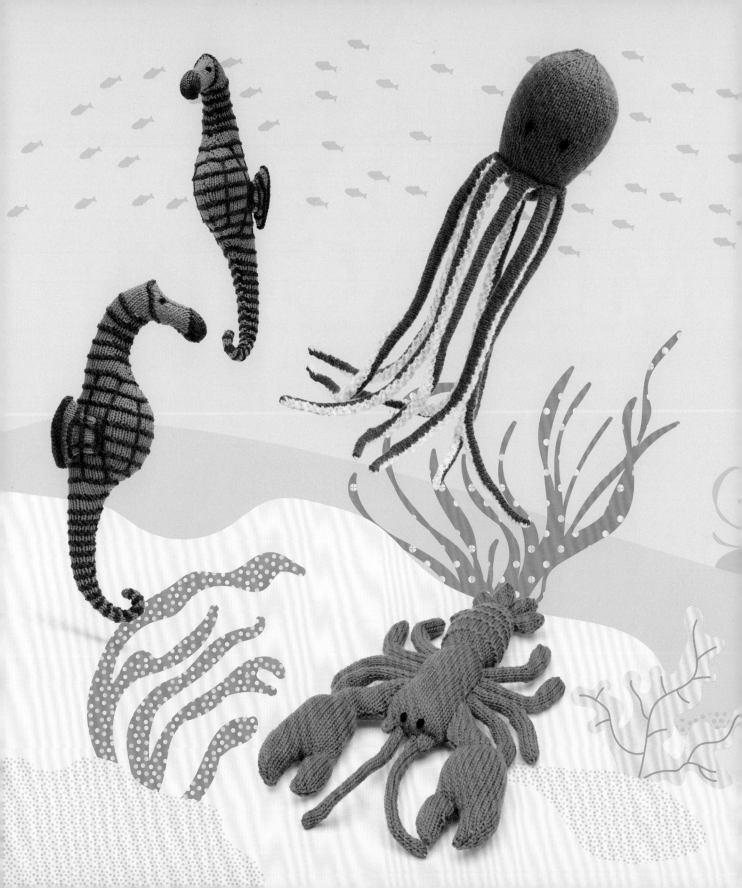

# Contents

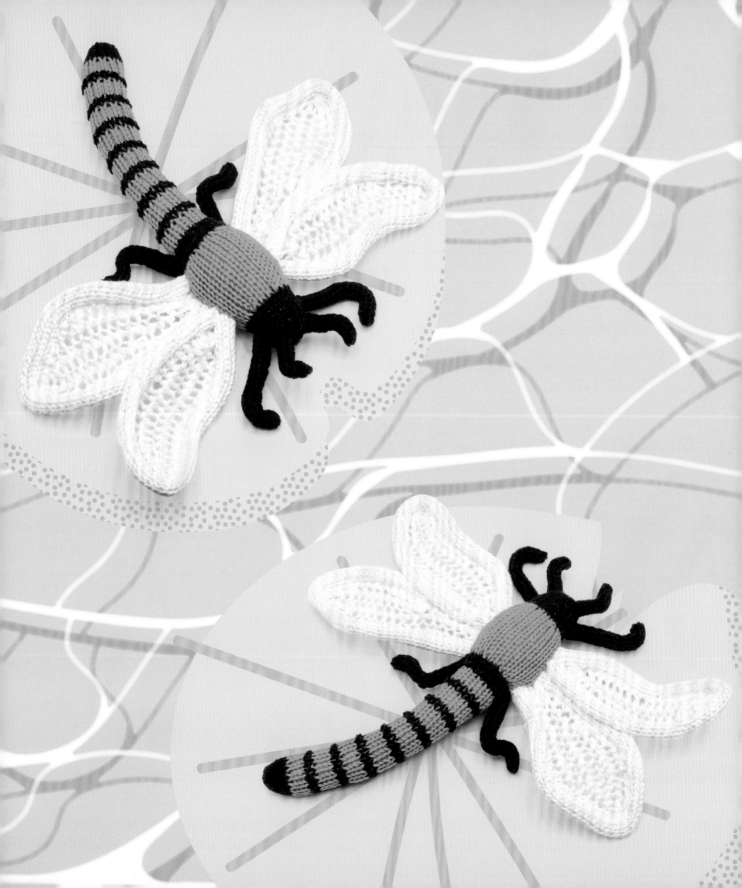

# Introduction

Working on the designs for this book has been a happy time for me. Patterns for 30 different animals are featured, some with their cute and cuddly offspring included too. The puffin and puffling are a favourite of mine, as are the adorable family of Guinea pigs and also the hedgehog family, which look prickly but actually are very soft. I hope there's something that will appeal to everyone in this varied collection, and wish you much satisfaction and enjoyment with whichever animals you decide to create.

Sarah Keen

LEFT TO RIGHT
LOVEBIRDS » 128
BLUE JAY » 98

LEFT TO RIGHT
DUCK-BILLED PLATYPUS » 80
KANGAROO WITH JOEY » 34

LEFT TO RIGHT
TROPICAL TREE FROG ➤➤ 124
LIZARD ➤➤ 136

# Lion

# Information you'll need

## Materials

Any DK (US: light worsted) yarn
(amounts given are approximate)
**Yarn A** mustard (60g)
**Yarn B** terracotta (30g)
**Yarn C** cream (5g)
**Yarn D** dark brown (2g)
Oddment of black for embroidery and terracotta
for making up
1 pair of 3.25mm (UK10:US3) needles
Knitters' pins and a blunt-ended needle for sewing up
Tweezers (optional)
Acrylic toy stuffing
1 chenille stem

## Finished size

Lion measures 7in (18cm) high

## Tension

26 sts x 34 rows measure 4in (10cm) square over st-st
using 3.25mm needles and DK yarn before stuffing,
or needles to give correct tension.

## Abbreviations

See page 164

# How to make Lion

## Body
Using the long tail method and yarn A, cast on 34 sts.
**Row 1 and foll alt row:** Purl.
**Row 2:** K10, (kfb) 14 times, k10 (48 sts).
**Row 4:** K16, (kfb, k2) 6 times, k14 (54 sts).
**Rows 5 to 17:** Beg with a p row, work 13 rows in st-st.
**Rows 18 and 19:** Cast off 10 sts at beg of next 2 rows (34 sts).
**Rows 20 to 35:** Work 16 rows in st-st.
**Rows 36 and 37:** Cast on 10 sts at beg of next 2 rows (54 sts).
**Rows 38 to 53:** Work 16 rows in st-st.
**Row 54:** K16, (k2tog, k2) 6 times, k14 (48 sts).
**Row 55:** Purl.
**Row 56:** K10, (k2tog) 14 times, k10 (34 sts).
**Rows 57 to 69:** Beg with a p row, work 13 rows in st-st.
**Rows 70 and 71:** Cast off 10 sts at beg of next 2 rows (14 sts).
**Rows 72 to 87:** Work 16 rows in st-st.
**Rows 88 and 89:** Cast on 10 sts at beg of next 2 rows (34 sts).
**Rows 90 to 105:** Work 16 rows in st-st. Cast off.

## Paws (make 4)
Using the long tail method and yarn B, cast on 24 sts and beg in g-st.
**Rows 1 to 6:** Work 6 rows in g-st.
**Rows 7 and 8:** P 2 rows for fold line.
**Row 9:** (K2tog, k1) to end (16 sts).
**Row 10:** Purl.
**Row 11:** (K2tog) to end (8 sts).
Break yarn and thread through sts on needle, pull tight and secure by threading yarn a second time through sts.

## Head and mane
Using the long tail method and yarn A, cast on 10 sts.
**Row 1 and foll 3 alt rows:** Purl.
**Row 2:** K1, (m1, k1) to end (19 sts).
**Row 4:** K1, (m1, k2) to end (28 sts).
**Row 6:** K1, (m1, k3) to end (37 sts).
**Row 8:** K1, (m1, k4) to end (46 sts).
**Rows 9 to 11:** Beg with a p row, work 3 rows in st-st.
Change to yarn B, cont in g-st and work mane:
**Row 12:** K2tog, k3, turn and work in g-st on these 4 sts.
**Row 13:** K1, m1, k2, m1, k1 (6 sts).
**Rows 14 to 43:** Work 30 rows in g-st.
**Row 44:** Cast off 5 sts, 1 st rem on RH needle, place this st onto LH needle and k2tog, k3, turn and work on these 4 sts.
**Row 45:** K1, m1, k2, m1, k1 (6 sts).
**Rows 46 to 75:** Work 30 rows in g-st.
**Rows 76 to 331:** Rep rows 44 to 75, 8 times more.
**Row 332:** Cast off 5 sts, 1 st rem on RH needle, place this st onto LH needle and k2tog, k2, k2tog, turn and work on these 4 sts.
**Row 333:** K1, m1, k2, m1, k1 (6 sts).
**Rows 334 to 363:** Work 30 rows in g-st. Cast off in g-st.

## Face
Using the long tail method and yarn A, cast on 10 sts.
**Row 1 and foll 3 alt rows:** Purl.
**Row 2:** K1, (m1, k1) to end (19 sts).
**Row 4:** K1, (m1, k2) to end (28 sts).
**Row 6:** K1, (m1, k3) to end (37 sts).
**Row 8:** K1, (m1, k4) to end (46 sts).
**Rows 9 to 15:** Beg with a p row, work 7 rows in st-st. Cast off.

## Snout (make 2 pieces)

Using the long tail method and yarn C, cast on 20 sts.

**Row 1 and foll alt row:** Purl.
**Row 2:** (K2tog, k2) to end (15 sts).
**Row 4:** (K2tog, k1) to end (10 sts).
Break yarn and thread through sts on needle, pull tight and secure by threading yarn a second time through sts.

## Nose

Using the long tail method and yarn D, cast on 8 sts.

**Rows 1 to 3:** Beg with a p row, work 3 rows in st-st.
**Row 4:** K1, k2tog, k2, k2tog, k1 (6 sts).
**Row 5 and foll alt row:** Purl.
**Row 6:** K1, (k2tog) twice, k1 (4 sts).
**Row 8:** K2tog, k2tog tbl (2 sts).
Break yarn and thread through sts on needle, pull tight and secure by threading yarn a second time through sts.

## Ears (make 2)

Using the long tail method and yarn A, cast on 7 sts.

**Row 1:** Purl.
**Row 2:** K1, (m1, k1) to end (13 sts).
**Rows 3 to 7:** Beg with a p row, work 5 rows in st-st.
**Row 8:** K1, (k2tog, k1) to end (9 sts).
Break yarn and thread through sts on needle, pull tight and secure by threading yarn a second time through sts.

## Tail

Using the long tail method and yarn A, cast on 15 sts.

**Rows 1 to 11:** Beg with a p row, work 11 rows in st-st.
Cast off.

# Making up Lion

**Note:** Sew up all row-end seams on right side using mattress stitch one stitch in from the edge, unless otherwise stated; a one-stitch seam allowance has been allowed for this.

## Body

Bring cast-on and cast-off stitches together and sew around legs and tummy. Sew up cast-on and cast-off stitches leaving a gap in the middle, stuff legs and body then sew up gap.

## Paws

Sew up side edges of paws and place around ends of feet. Sew cast-on stitches of paws to legs using back stitch on right side all the way round.

## Head, mane and face

Sew cast-off stitches of mane down. Gather round cast-on stitches of back of head and face, pull tight and secure then sew up row ends. Pin and sew outside edge of face to first row of mane all the way round by taking a short stitch over one stitch of mane, then a short stitch over one stitch of face and do this alternately all the way round leaving a gap. Stuff and sew up gap. Pin and sew head to body.

## Snout, nose and features

Sew up row ends of two pieces of snout, place these two side by side and sew together at centre. Using picture as a guide, pin and sew snout to lower half of head leaving a gap, stuff snout with tweezers or tip of scissors and sew up gap. Sew side edges of nose to centre of snout, stuff from top edge and sew top edge to face. Mark position of eyes with two pins and embroider eyes in black making a vertical chain stitch for each eye, then a second chain stitch on top of first (see page 163 for how to begin and fasten off invisibly for the embroidery).

## Ears

Sew up side edges of ears and with this seam at centre back, position and sew ears to head.

## Tail

Make a tassel using terracotta by winding yarn round two fingers 30 times. Cut through all strands, tie a piece of yarn around centre and fold tassel in half. Attach base of tassel to one end of inside edge of tail, fold chenille stem in half and place on wrong side of tail and sew up side edges of tail enclosing chenille stem inside. Cut chenille stem to length of tail. Trim ends of tassel to 1in (2.5cm). Bend tail and sew to Lion.

# Orangutan with Infant

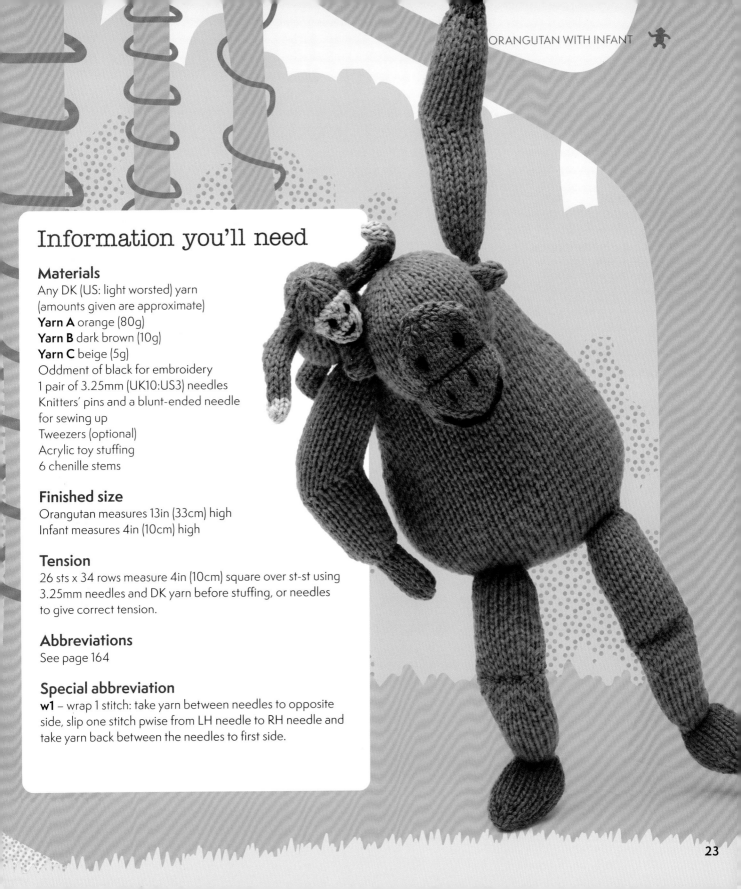

# Information you'll need

## Materials
Any DK (US: light worsted) yarn
(amounts given are approximate)
**Yarn A** orange (80g)
**Yarn B** dark brown (10g)
**Yarn C** beige (5g)
Oddment of black for embroidery
1 pair of 3.25mm (UK10:US3) needles
Knitters' pins and a blunt-ended needle
for sewing up
Tweezers (optional)
Acrylic toy stuffing
6 chenille stems

## Finished size
Orangutan measures 13in (33cm) high
Infant measures 4in (10cm) high

## Tension
26 sts x 34 rows measure 4in (10cm) square over st-st using
3.25mm needles and DK yarn before stuffing, or needles
to give correct tension.

## Abbreviations
See page 164

## Special abbreviation
**w1** – wrap 1 stitch: take yarn between needles to opposite
side, slip one stitch pwise from LH needle to RH needle and
take yarn back between the needles to first side.

# How to make Orangutan

## Body

Using the long tail method and yarn A, cast on 32 sts and place a marker at centre of cast-on edge.

**Row 1 and foll 4 alt rows:** Purl.
**Row 2:** *K5, (m1, k2) 4 times, k3; rep from * once (40 sts).
**Row 4:** *K7, (m1, k2) 4 times, k5; rep from * once (48 sts).
**Row 6:** *K9, (m1, k2) 4 times, k7; rep from * once (56 sts).
**Row 8:** *K11, (m1, k2) 4 times, k9; rep from * once (64 sts).
**Row 10:** *K13, (m1, k2) 4 times, k11; rep from * once (72 sts).
**Rows 11 to 29:** Work 19 rows in st-st.
**Row 30:** K16, (k2tog) twice, k32, (k2tog) twice, k16 (68 sts).
**Rows 31 to 33:** Work 3 rows in st-st.
**Row 34:** K15, (k2tog) twice, k30, (k2tog) twice, k15 (64 sts).
**Rows 35 to 37:** Work 3 rows in st-st.
**Row 38:** K14, (k2tog) twice, k28, (k2tog) twice, k14 (60 sts).
**Rows 39 to 41:** Work 3 rows in st-st.
**Row 42:** K13, (k2tog) twice, k26, (k2tog) twice, k13 (56 sts).
**Rows 43 to 45:** Work 3 rows in st-st.
**Row 46:** K12, (k2tog) twice, k24, (k2tog) twice, k12 (52 sts).
**Rows 47 to 49:** Work 3 rows in st-st.
**Row 50:** K11, (k2tog) twice, k22, (k2tog) twice, k11 (48 sts).
**Row 51:** Purl.
**Row 52:** K22, cast off 4 sts (23 sts now on RH needle) k21 (44 sts).
**Row 53:** P20, p2tog, turn and work on these 21 sts.
**Row 54:** K2tog, k to end (20 sts).
**Row 55:** Purl.
**Rows 56 and 57:** Rep rows 54 and 55 once (19 sts).
**Row 58:** (K2tog, k2) 3 times, k7 (16 sts).
**Row 59:** Purl.
**Row 60:** K2, (k2tog) 4 times, k6 (12 sts).
**Row 61:** P4, (p2tog) 4 times (8 sts). Cast off.
**Row 62:** Rejoin yarn to rem sts, p2tog, p to end (21 sts).
**Row 63:** K to last 2 sts, k2tog (20 sts).
**Row 64:** Purl.
**Rows 65 and 66:** Rep rows 63 and 64 once (19 sts).
**Row 67:** K9, (k2tog, k2) twice, k2tog (16 sts).
**Row 68:** Purl.
**Row 69:** K6, (k2tog) 4 times, k2 (12 sts).
**Row 70:** (P2tog) 4 times, p4 (8 sts). Cast off.

## Head

Using the long tail method and yarn A, cast on 9 sts.

**Row 1 and foll 2 alt rows:** Purl.
**Row 2:** K1, (m1, k1) to end (17 sts).
**Row 4:** K1, (m1, k2) to end (25 sts).
**Row 6:** K1, (m1, k3) to end (33 sts).
**Rows 7 to 9:** Work 3 rows in st-st.
**Row 10:** K1, (m1, k4) to end (41 sts).
**Rows 11 to 25:** Work 15 rows in st-st.
**Row 26:** K1, (k2tog, k3) to end (33 sts).
**Row 27 and foll 2 alt rows:** Purl.
**Row 28:** K1, (k2tog, k2) to end (25 sts).
**Row 30:** K1, (k2tog, k1) to end (17 sts).
**Row 32:** K1, (k2tog) to end (9 sts).
Break yarn and thread through sts on needle, pull tight and secure by threading yarn a second time through sts.

## Muzzle

Using the long tail method and yarn B, cast on 28 sts.
**Row 1:** Purl.
**Row 2:** K4, (m1, k4) to end (34 sts).
**Rows 3 to 5:** Work 3 rows in st-st.
**Row 6:** *K3, (k2tog, k1) 4 times, k2; rep from * once (26 sts).
**Row 7 and foll alt row:** Purl.
**Row 8:** *K2, (k2tog) twice, k1, (k2tog) twice, k2; rep from * once (18 sts).
**Row 10:** (K2tog) to end (9 sts).
Break yarn and thread through sts on needle, pull tight and secure by threading yarn a second time through sts.

## Face piece

Using the long tail method and yarn B, cast on 12 sts.
**Row 1:** Purl.
**Row 2:** K1, m1, k10, m1, k1 (14 sts).
**Rows 3 to 7:** Beg with a p row, work 5 rows in st-st.
**Row 8:** (K2tog) twice, k6, (k2tog) twice (10 sts).
**Row 9:** Purl.
**Row 10:** (K2tog) to end (5 sts).
**Row 11:** Purl.
Break yarn and thread through sts on needle, pull tight and secure by threading yarn a second time through sts.

## Ears (make 2)

Using the long tail method and yarn A, cast on 12 sts.
**Rows 1 to 3:** Beg with a p row, work 3 rows in st-st.
**Row 4:** (K2tog) to end (6 sts).
Break yarn and thread through sts on needle, pull tight and secure by threading yarn a second time through sts.

## Legs (make 2)

Using the long tail method and yarn A, cast on 11 sts.

**Row 1:** Purl.

**Row 2:** K1, (m1, k1) to end (21 sts).

**Rows 3 to 21:** Beg with a p row, work 19 rows in st-st.

Place a marker on first and last st of last row and on centre stitch and keep markers on RS.

**Rows 22 to 27:** Work 6 rows in st-st.

**Row 28:** K1, k2tog, k5, k2tog, k1, k2tog, k5, k2tog, k1 (17 sts).

**Rows 29 to 41:** Work 13 rows in st-st.

**Row 42:** K2tog, (k1, k2tog) to end (11 sts).

**Row 43:** Purl.

Cast off.

## Feet (make 2)

Using the long tail method and yarn B, cast on 12 sts.

**Row 1 and foll alt row:** Purl.

**Row 2:** (K1, m1, k4, m1, k1) twice (16 sts).

**Row 4:** (K1, m1, k6, m1, k1) twice (20 sts).

**Rows 5 to 11:** Work 7 rows in st-st.

**Shape big toe:**

**Row 12:** K6, (k2tog) 4 times, k6 (16 sts).

**Row 13:** P7, p2tog, p7 (15 sts).

**Rows 14 to 17:** Work 4 rows in st-st.

**Row 18:** K1, (k2tog) 3 times, k1, (k2tog) 3 times, k1 (9 sts)

**Row 19:** Purl.

Break yarn and thread through sts on needle, pull tight and secure by threading yarn a second time through sts.

## Arms (make 2)

Using the long tail method and yarn A, cast on 10 sts.

**Row 1:** Purl.

**Row 2:** K1, (m1, k1) to end (19 sts).

**Rows 3 to 17:** Beg with a p row, work 15 rows in st-st.

**Row 18:** K8, w1 (see special abbreviation), turn.

**Row 19:** S1p, p to end.

**Row 20:** K7, w1, turn.

**Row 21:** S1p, p to end.

**Row 22:** K6, w1, turn.

**Row 23:** S1p, p to end.

**Row 24:** K5, w1, turn.

**Row 25:** S1p, p to end.

**Row 26:** K4, w1, turn.

**Row 27:** S1p, p to end.

**Row 28:** K3, w1, turn.

**Row 29:** S1p, p to end.

**Row 30:** K across all sts.

**Row 31:** P8, w1, turn.

**Row 32:** S1k, k to end.

**Row 33:** P7, w1, turn.

**Row 34:** S1k, k to end.

**Row 35:** P6, w1, turn.

**Row 36:** S1k, k to end.

**Row 37:** P5, w1, turn.

**Row 38:** S1k, k to end.

**Row 39:** P4, w1, turn.

**Row 40:** S1k, k to end.

**Row 41:** P3, w1, turn.

**Row 42:** S1k, k to end.

**Rows 43 to 53:** Work 11 rows in st-st.

**Row 54:** K1, k2tog, k13, k2tog, k1 (17 sts).

**Row 55:** Purl.

**Row 56:** K2tog, (k1, k2tog) to end (11 sts).

**Row 57:** Purl.

Cast off.

## Hands (make 2)

Using the long tail method and yarn B, cast on 12 sts.

**Rows 1 to 7:** Beg with a p row, work 7 rows in st-st.

**Row 8:** (K1, k2tog) twice, (k2tog, k1) twice (8 sts).

**Row 9:** Purl.

Break yarn and thread through sts on needle, pull tight and secure by threading yarn a second time through sts.

# Making up Orangutan

**Note:** Sew up all row-end seams on right side using mattress stitch one stitch in from the edge, unless otherwise stated; a one-stitch seam allowance has been allowed for this.

## Body and head

Sew up side edges of body, bring marker and seam together at base and oversew cast-on stitches. Leaving neck open, stuff body. Gather round cast-on stitches of head, pull tight and sew up side edges of head leaving a gap. Stuff head and sew up gap. Place head into top of body and pin cast-on stitches to centre of chest. Sew head to body making a short horizontal stitch from head then a short horizontal stitch from body and do this alternately all the way round.

## Muzzle

Sew up side edges of muzzle and stuff. Pin and sew muzzle to lower half of head at centre front.

## Face piece

Sew face piece to head, sitting it on top of muzzle using back stitch around outside edge.

## Ears

Sew up row ends of ears and sew ears to sides of head.

## Features

Using picture as a guide, mark position of eyes with two pins and embroider eyes in black making a vertical chain stitch for each eye, then a second chain stitch on top of first. Embroider two nostrils in black using straight stitches and mouth in black using stem stitch (see page 163 for how to begin and fasten off invisibly for the embroidery).

## Legs and feet

Fold cast-on stitches of legs in half and oversew. Sew up side edges of legs from cast-on stitches to markers. Stuff upper legs and sew a running stitch at knee from markers at side to marker in the middle and back to the side again. Finish sewing up side edges leaving a gap, stuff and sew up gap. Fold cast-on stitches of feet in half and oversew. Sew up side edges of feet leaving a gap, stuff and sew up gap. Sew feet to legs with big toes pointing inwards. Sew legs to body.

## Arms and hands

Fold cast-off stitches of arms in half and oversew. Sew up side edges of arms from stitches pulled tight on a thread to elbow, and stuff this part. Finish sewing up side edges of arms leaving a gap, stuff and sew up gap. Sew up side edges of hands, bend a double chenille stem into a 'u' shape and insert into each hand. Cut excess chenille stem and sew hands to ends of arms. Sew top of arms to body at either side.

## How to make Infant Orangutan

### Body and head
Using the long tail method and yarn A, cast on 9 sts.
**Row 1 and foll alt row:** Purl.
**Row 2:** K1, (m1, k1) to end (17 sts).
**Row 4:** K1, (m1, k2) to end (25 sts).
**Rows 5 to 13:** Work 9 rows in st-st.
**Row 14:** K4, (k2tog) 3 times, k5, (k2tog) 3 times, k4 (19 sts).
**Rows 15 to 17:** Work 3 rows in st-st.
**Row 18:** K1, (k2tog, k1) to end (13 sts).
**Row 19:** Purl.
**Row 20:** (K1, m1, k3, m1) 3 times, k1 (19 sts).
**Rows 21 to 27:** Work 7 rows in st-st.
**Row 28:** K1, (k2tog, k1) to end (13 sts).
**Row 29:** Purl.
**Row 30:** K1, (k2tog, k1) to end (9 sts).
Break yarn, thread through sts on needle and leave loose.

### Face piece
Using the long tail method and yarn C, cast on 12 sts.
**Row 1:** Purl.
**Row 2:** K2, (k2tog) 4 times, k2 (8 sts).
**Row 3:** P2, (p2tog) twice, p2 (6 sts).
Break yarn and thread through sts on needle, pull tight and secure by threading yarn a second time through sts.

### Muzzle
Using the long tail method and yarn C, cast on 14 sts.
**Rows 1 to 3:** Beg with a p row, work 3 rows in st-st.
**Row 4:** K1, (k2tog) 6 times, k1 (8 sts).
Break yarn and thread through sts on needle, pull tight and secure by threading yarn a second time through sts.

### Ears (make 2)
Using the long tail method and yarn A, cast on 8 sts.
Break yarn and thread through sts on needle, pull tight and secure by threading yarn a second time through sts.

### Arms and legs (make 4)
Using the long tail method and yarn A, cast on 12 sts.
**Rows 1 to 3:** Beg with a p row, work 3 rows in st-st.
**Row 4:** K2tog, k8, k2tog (10 sts).
**Rows 5 to 9:** Work 5 rows in st-st.
**Row 10:** K2tog, k6, k2tog (8 sts).
**Rows 11 to 13:** Work 3 rows in st-st.
**Rows 14 to 17:** Change to yarn C and work 4 rows in st-st.
Break yarn and thread through sts on needle, pull tight and secure by threading yarn a second time through sts.

## Making up Infant Orangutan

**Note:** Sew up all row-end seams on right side using mattress stitch one stitch in from the edge, unless otherwise stated; a one-stitch seam allowance has been allowed for this.

### Body and head
Gather round cast-on stitches of body, pull tight and secure. Sew up row ends of body and head and stuff body and head. Pull stitches on a thread tight at top of head and fasten off.

### Face piece
Place face piece on face and sew all edges down.

### Muzzle
Sew up row ends of muzzle and place a small ball of stuffing into muzzle with tweezers or tip of scissors. Pin and sew muzzle to lower half of face.

### Features
Using picture as a guide, mark position of eyes with two pins and embroider eyes in black making a chain stitch for each eye. Make a small straight stitch for nose and embroider mouth using stem stitch (see page 163 for how to begin and fasten off the embroidery invisibly).

### Ears
Sew ears to sides of head.

### Arms and legs
Fold a chenille stem in half for each arm and leg and place folded end into stitches pulled tight on a thread. Sew up row ends of arms and legs enclosing chenille stems inside. Cut chenille stems to length of arms and legs and sew arms and legs to Infant Orangutan. Bend arms and legs.

# Elephant with Calf

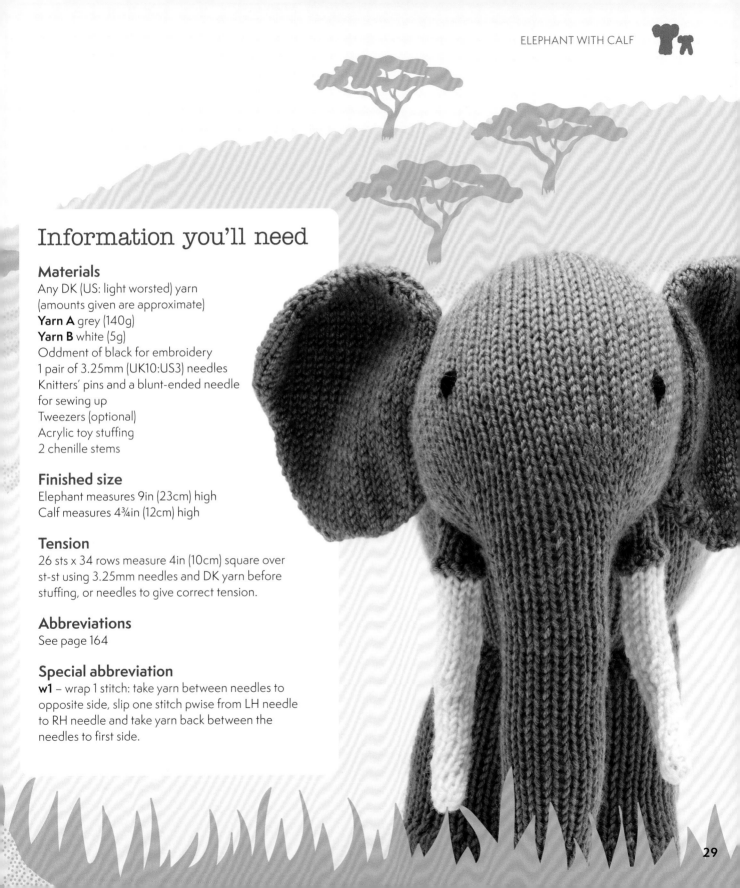

# Information you'll need

## Materials
Any DK (US: light worsted) yarn
(amounts given are approximate)
**Yarn A** grey (140g)
**Yarn B** white (5g)
Oddment of black for embroidery
1 pair of 3.25mm (UK10:US3) needles
Knitters' pins and a blunt-ended needle
for sewing up
Tweezers (optional)
Acrylic toy stuffing
2 chenille stems

## Finished size
Elephant measures 9in (23cm) high
Calf measures 4¾in (12cm) high

## Tension
26 sts x 34 rows measure 4in (10cm) square over
st-st using 3.25mm needles and DK yarn before
stuffing, or needles to give correct tension.

## Abbreviations
See page 164

## Special abbreviation
**w1** – wrap 1 stitch: take yarn between needles to
opposite side, slip one stitch pwise from LH needle
to RH needle and take yarn back between the
needles to first side.

# How to make Elephant

## Body

### Right side
Using the long tail method and yarn A, cast on 38 sts.
**Row 1 and foll 2 alt rows:** Purl.
**Row 2:** (K2, m1) twice, k30, (m1, k2) twice (42 sts).
**Row 4:** (K2, m1) twice, k34, (m1, k2) twice (46 sts).
**Row 6:** (K2, m1) twice, k38, (m1, k2) twice (50 sts).
**Rows 7 to 29:** Work 23 rows in st-st.**
**Row 30:** Cast off 4 sts kwise, k to end (46 sts).
**Row 31:** Purl.
**Row 32:** K2tog, k to end (45 sts).
**Row 33:** P to last 2 sts, p2tog (44 sts).
**Rows 34 to 37:** Rep rows 32 and 33 twice more (40 sts).
**Rows 38 to 39:** Work 2 rows in st-st.
**Row 40:** K to last 2 sts, k2tog (39 sts).
**Row 41:** Purl.
**Row 42:** As row 40 (38 sts).
**Row 43:** P2tog, p to end (37 sts).
**Row 44:** K to last 2 sts, k2tog (36 sts).
**Rows 45 and 48:** Rep rows 43 and 44 twice more (32 sts).
**Row 49:** Cast off 4 sts pwise, p to end (28 sts).
**Row 50:** Knit.
**Rows 51 to 60:** Rep rows 49 and 50, 5 times more (8 sts).
Cast off pwise.

### Left side
Work as for right side from beg to **.
**Row 30:** K46, cast off rem 4 sts and fasten off (46 sts).
**Row 31:** Rejoin yarn to rem sts and p 1 row.
**Row 32:** K to last 2 sts, k2tog (45 sts).

**Row 33:** P2tog, p to end (44 sts).
**Rows 34 to 37:** Rep rows 32 and 33 twice more (40 sts).
**Rows 38 and 39:** Work 2 rows in st-st.
**Row 40:** K2tog, k to end (39 sts).
**Row 41:** Purl.
**Row 42:** As row 40 (38 sts).
**Row 43:** P to last 2 sts, p2tog (37 sts).
**Row 44:** K2tog, k to end (36 sts).
**Rows 45 to 48:** Rep rows 43 and 44 twice more (32 sts).
**Row 49:** Purl.
**Row 50:** Cast off 4 sts, k to end (28 sts).
**Row 51:** Purl.
**Rows 52 to 61:** Rep rows 50 and 51, 5 times more (8 sts)
Cast off.

## Trunk and head
Using the long tail method and yarn A, cast on 20 sts.
**Row 1 and foll alt row:** Purl.
**Row 2:** (K1, m1, k8, m1, k1) twice (24 sts).
**Row 4:** (K1, m1, k10, m1, k1) twice (28 sts).
**Rows 5 to 9:** Beg with a p row, work 5 rows in st-st.
**Row 10:** Cast off 6 sts (1 st now on RH needle), k6, m1, k2, m1, k7, cast off 6 rem sts and fasten off.
**Row 11:** Rejoin yarn to rem sts and p to end (18 sts).
**Row 12:** K1, m1, k to last st, m1, k1 (20 sts).
**Rows 13 to 45:** Beg with a p row, work 33 rows in st-st.
**Row 46:** (K1, m1) 4 times, k12, (m1, k1)

4 times (28 sts).
**Row 47 and foll 3 alt rows:** Purl.
**Row 48:** (K2, m1) 4 times, k12, (m1, k2) 4 times (36 sts).
**Row 50:** (K3, m1) 4 times, k12, (m1, k3) 4 times (44 sts).
**Row 52:** (K4, m1) 4 times, k12, (m1, k4) 4 times (52 sts).
**Row 54:** (K5, m1) 4 times, k12, (m1, k5) 4 times (60 sts).
**Rows 55 to 79:** Work 25 rows in st-st.
**Row 80:** (K2tog, k4) to end (50 sts).
**Row 81 and foll 3 alt rows:** Purl.
**Row 82:** (K2tog, k3) to end (40 sts).
**Row 84:** (K2tog, k2) to end (30 sts).
**Row 86:** (K2tog, k1) to end (20 sts).
**Row 88:** (K2tog) to end (10 sts).
Break yarn and thread through sts on needle, pull tight and secure by threading yarn a second time through sts.

## Legs (make 2 right legs and 2 left legs following individual instructions)

Using the long tail method and yarn A, cast on 10 sts.
**Row 1 and foll 2 alt rows:** Purl.
**Row 2:** K1, (kfb) to end (19 sts).
**Row 4:** K1, (kfb, k1) to end (28 sts).
**Row 6:** K9, (m1, k2) 6 times, k7 (34 sts).
**Rows 7 to 10:** Work 4 rows in st-st ending on a k row.
**Row 11:** P11, (p2tog) 6 times, p11 (28 sts).
**Rows 12 to 29:** Work 18 rows in st-st.
**Row 30 For right leg:** K24, w1 (see special abbreviation), turn.
**Row 30 For left leg:** K14, w1, turn.
**Row 31:** S1p, p10, w1, turn.
**Row 32:** S1k, k8, w1, turn.
**Row 33:** S1p, p6, w1, turn.
**Row 34:** S1k, k to end.
**Row 35:** Purl.
Cast off.

## Ears (make 2)

Using the long tail method and A, cast on 16 sts.
**Row 1 and foll 3 alt rows:** Purl.
**Row 2:** *(K1, m1) twice, k4, (m1, k1) twice; rep from * once (24 sts).
**Row 4:** *(K1, m1) twice, k8, (m1, k1) twice; rep from * once (32 sts).
**Row 6:** *(K1, m1) twice, k12, (m1, k1) twice; rep from * once (40 sts).
**Row 8:** *(K1, m1) twice, k16, (m1, k1) twice; rep from * once (48 sts).
**Rows 9 to 17:** Work 9 rows in st-st.
**Row 18:** K22, k2tog tbl, k2tog, k22 (46 sts).
**Row 19 and foll 2 alt rows:** Purl.
**Row 20:** K21, k2tog tbl, k2tog, k21 (44 sts).
**Row 22:** K20, k2tog tbl, k2tog, k20 (42 sts).
**Row 24:** K19, k2tog tbl, k2tog, k19 (40 sts).
**Rows 25 to 29:** Work 5 rows in st-st.
**Row 30:** (K2tog) twice, k14, k2tog tbl, k2tog, k14, k2tog, k2tog tbl (34 sts).
**Row 31 and foll 2 alt rows:** Purl.
**Row 32:** (K2tog) twice, k11, k2tog tbl, k2tog, k11, k2tog, k2tog tbl (28 sts).
**Row 34:** (K2tog) twice, k8, k2tog tbl, k2tog, k8, k2tog, k2tog tbl (22 sts).
**Row 36:** (K2tog) twice, k5, k2tog tbl, k2tog, k5, k2tog, k2tog tbl (16 sts).
Cast off pwise.

## Tusks (make 2)

Using the long tail method and yarn A, cast on 9 sts.
**Rows 1 to 5:** Beg with a p row, work 5 rows in st-st.
**Row 6:** K1, (m1, k1) to end (17 sts).
**Row 7:** Knit.
Change to yarn B and dec:
**Row 8:** K2tog, (k1, k2tog) to end (11 sts).
**Rows 9 to 19:** Beg with a p row, work 11 rows in st-st.
**Row 20:** K4, k2tog, k5 (10 sts).
**Row 21:** Purl.

**Row 22:** K4, k2tog, k4 (9 sts).
**Rows 23 to 29:** Work 7 rows in st-st.
**Row 30:** K3, k2tog, k4 (8 sts).
**Row 31 and foll alt row:** Purl.
**Row 32:** K3, k2tog, k3 (7 sts).
**Row 34:** K1, (k2tog, k1) twice (5 sts).
Break yarn and thread through sts on needle, pull tight and secure by threading yarn a second time through sts.

## Tail

Using the long tail method and A, cast on 20 sts.
**Rows 1 to 7:** Beg with a p row, work 7 rows in st-st.
Cast off.

# Making up Elephant

**Note:** Sew up all row-end seams on right side using mattress stitch one stitch in from the edge, unless otherwise stated; a one-stitch seam allowance has been allowed for this.

## Body

Place two halves of body together matching all edges and sew around outside edge leaving neck open, then stuff.

## Trunk and head

Fold cast-on stitches of trunk in half and sew together. Sew up row ends of trunk and stuff trunk. Sew up row ends of head leaving a gap, stuff head and sew up gap. Pin and sew head to neck of body.

## Legs

Gather round cast-on stitches of legs, pull tight and secure. Sew up side edges and stuff legs. Sew legs to Elephant.

## Ears

Fold cast-on stitches of ears in half and sew up. Fold cast-off stitches in half and sew up. Sew up side edges and sew ears to sides of head.

## Tusks

Fold a chenille stem in half and place fold into stitches pulled tight on a thread. Sew up side edges of tusks enclosing chenille stems inside, stuff wide part with tweezers or tip of scissors and cut excess chenille stems. Sew tusks to Elephant and curl forward.

## Tail

Make a tassel using grey by winding yarn round two fingers ten times. Cut through all strands, tie a piece of yarn around centre and fold tassel in half. Attach base of tassel to one end of inside edge of tail and sew up cast-on and cast-off stitches of tail along its length. Trim tassel to ¾in (2cm). Sew tail to Elephant.

## Features

Using picture as a guide, mark position of eyes with two pins at top of trunk and embroider eyes in black making a vertical chain stitch for each eye, then a second chain stitch on top of first (see page 163 for how to begin and fasten off invisibly for the embroidery).

## How to make Elephant Calf

### Body

**Right side**

Using the long tail method and yarn A, cast on 14 sts.

**Row 1 and foll 2 alt rows:** Purl.
**Row 2:** (K2, m1) twice, k6, (m1, k2) twice (18 sts).
**Row 4:** (K2, m1) twice, k10, (m1, k2) twice (22 sts).
**Row 6:** (K2, m1) twice, k14, (m1, k2) twice (26 sts).
**Rows 7 to 15:** Beg with a p row, work 9 rows in st-st.**
**Row 16:** Cast off 3 sts, k to end (23 sts).
**Row 17:** Purl.

**Row 18:** K2tog, k to end (22 sts).
**Rows 19 to 22:** Rep rows 17 and 18 twice more (20 sts).
**Row 23:** Purl.
**Row 24:** K2tog, k to last 2 sts, k2tog (18 sts).
**Rows 25 and 26:** Rep rows 23 and 24 once (16 sts).
**Row 27:** Cast off 4 sts pwise, p to end (12 sts).
**Row 28:** Knit.
**Rows 29 to 32:** Rep rows 27 and 28 twice more (4 sts).
Cast off pwise.

**Left side**

**Rows 1 to 15:** Work as for right side from beg to **.
**Row 16:** K to last 3 sts, cast off 3 sts and fasten off (23 sts).
**Row 17:** Rejoin yarn and p to end.
**Row 18:** K to last 2 sts, k2tog (22 sts).
**Row 19:** Purl.
**Rows 20 to 23:** Rep rows 18 and 19 twice more (20 sts).
**Row 24:** K2tog, k to last 2 sts, k2tog (18 sts).
**Row 25:** Purl.
**Rows 26 and 27:** Rep rows 24 and 25 once (16 sts).
**Row 28:** Cast off 4 sts, k to end (12 sts).
**Row 29:** Purl.
**Rows 30 to 33:** Rep rows 28 and 29 twice more (4 sts).
Cast off.

## Trunk and head

Using the long tail method and yarn A, cast on 8 sts.
**Row 1:** Purl.
**Row 2:** K1, (m1, k2) 3 times, m1, k1 (12 sts).
**Rows 3 to 13:** Beg with a p row, work 11 rows in st-st.
**Row 14:** K1, (m1, k2) to last st, m1, k1 (18 sts).
**Row 15:** Purl.
**Row 16:** K4, (m1, k2) 6 times, k2 (24 sts).

**Rows 17 to 19:** Beg with a p row, work 3 rows in st-st.
**Row 20:** K6, (m1, k1) 6 times, (k1, m1) 6 times, k6 (36 sts).
**Rows 21 to 29:** Beg with a p row, work 9 rows in st-st.
**Row 30:** (K2tog, k4) to end (30 sts).
**Row 31 and foll 3 alt rows:** Purl.
**Row 32:** (K2tog, k3) to end (24 sts).
**Row 34:** (K2tog, k2) to end (18 sts).
**Row 36:** (K2tog, k1) to end (12 sts).
**Row 38:** (K2tog) to end (6 sts).
Break yarn and thread through sts on needle, pull tight and secure by threading yarn a second time through sts.

## Legs (make 4)

Using the long tail method and yarn A, cast on 8 sts.
**Row 1 and foll alt row:** Purl.
**Row 2:** (Kfb) to end (16 sts).
**Row 4:** (Kfb, k1) to end (24 sts).
**Rows 5 to 7:** Work 3 rows in st-st.
**Row 8:** K4, (k2tog) 8 times, k4 (16 sts).
**Rows 9 to 19:** Work 11 rows in st-st.
**Row 20:** (K2tog, k4, k2tog) twice (12 sts).
**Row 21:** Purl.
Cast off.

## Ears (make 2)

Using the long tail method and yarn A, cast on 14 sts.
**Row 1:** Purl.
**Row 2:** (K1, m1) twice, k4, m1, k2, m1, k4, (m1, k1) twice (20 sts).
**Rows 3 to 11:** Beg with a p row, work 9 rows in st-st.
**Row 12:** (K2tog, k6, k2tog) twice (16 sts).
**Row 13:** Purl.
**Row 14:** (K2tog) to end (8 sts).
Cast off pwise.

## Tail

Using the long tail method and yarn A, cast on 10 sts.
**Rows 1 to 7:** Beg with a p row, work 7 rows in st-st.
Cast off.

# Making up Elephant Calf

**Note:** Sew up all row-end seams on right side using mattress stitch one stitch in from the edge, unless otherwise stated; a one-stitch seam allowance has been allowed for this.

## Body

Place two halves of body together matching all edges and sew around outside edge leaving neck open. Stuff body.

## Trunk and head

Gather round cast-on stitches of trunk, pull tight and secure. Sew up row ends of trunk and stuff trunk with tweezers or tip of scissors. Sew up row ends of head leaving a gap, stuff head and sew up gap. Pin and sew head to neck of body.

## Legs

Fold cast-off stitches in half and sew up. Gather round cast-on stitches, pull tight and secure. Sew up side edges leaving a gap, stuff and sew up gap. Pin and sew legs to Calf.

## Ears

Fold ears bringing side edges together and sew around open edges. Sew ears to Calf.

## Tail

Make a tassel using grey by winding yarn round two fingers eight times. Cut through all strands, tie a piece of yarn around centre and fold tassel in half. Attach base of tassel to one end of inside edge of tail and sew up cast-on and cast-off stitches of tail along its length. Trim tassel to ½in (13mm) and sew tail to Calf.

## Features

Using picture as a guide, mark position of eyes with two pins at top of trunk and embroider eyes in black making a vertical chain stitch for each eye, then a second chain stitch on top of first (see page 163 for how to begin and fasten off invisibly for the embroidery).

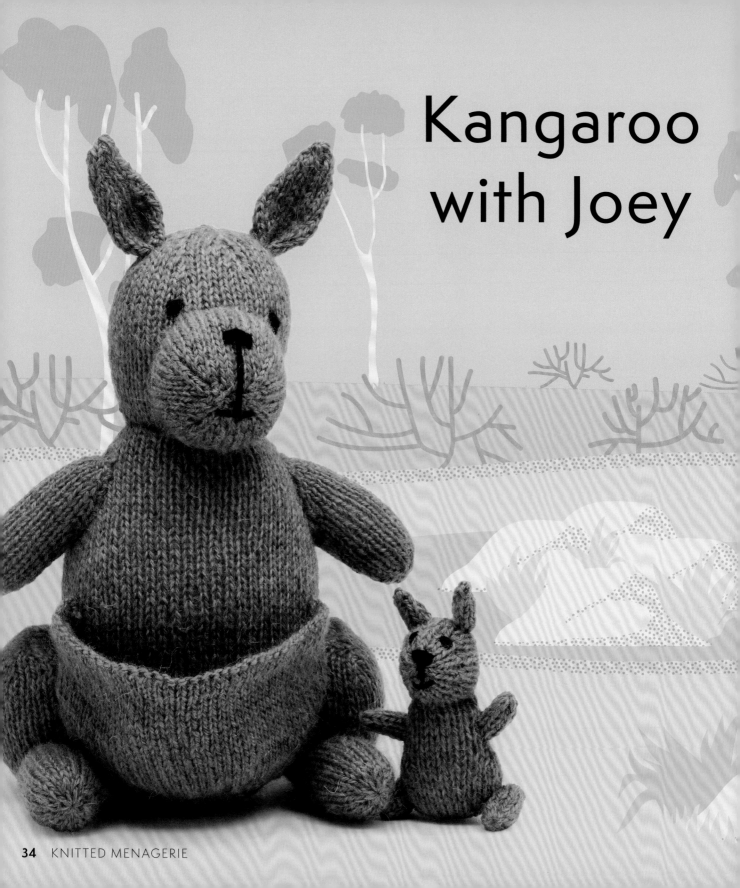

# Kangaroo with Joey

# Information you'll need

## Materials

Any DK (US: light worsted) yarn
(amounts given are approximate)
**Yarn A** ginger (120g)
Oddment of black for embroidery
1 pair of 3.25mm (UK10:US3) needles
Knitters' pins and a blunt-ended needle for sewing up
Acrylic toy stuffing

## Finished size

Kangaroo measures 10in (25.5cm) high
Joey measures 3½in (9cm) high

## Tension

26 sts x 34 rows measure 4in (10cm) square over st-st
using 3.25mm needles and DK yarn before stuffing, or
needles to give correct tension.

## Abbreviations

See page 164

## Special abbreviation

**w1** – wrap 1 stitch: take yarn between needles to
opposite side, slip one stitch pwise from LH needle
to RH needle and take yarn back between the
needles to first side.

# How to make Kangaroo

## Body
Using the long tail method and yarn A, cast on 8 sts.

**Row 1 and foll 6 alt rows:** Purl.
**Row 2:** (Kfb) to end (16 sts).
**Row 4:** *K1, (kfb) twice, k1; rep from * 3 times more (24 sts).
**Row 6:** *K2, (kfb) twice, k2; rep from * 3 times more (32 sts).
**Row 8:** *K3, (kfb) twice, k3; rep from * 3 times more (40 sts).
**Row 10:** *K4, (kfb) twice, k4; rep from * 3 times more (48 sts).
**Row 12:** *K5, (kfb) twice, k5; rep from * 3 times more (56 sts).
**Row 14:** *K6, (kfb) twice, k6; rep from * 3 times more (64 sts).
**Row 15:** Purl.
**Mark position for sewing on pouch:**
**Row 16:** K20, p1, k22, p1, k20.
**Row 17:** Purl.
**Rows 18 to 41:** Rep rows 16 and 17, 12 times more.
**Rows 42 to 51:** Work 10 rows in st-st.
**Row 52:** *K14, (k2tog) twice, k14; rep from * once (60 sts).
**Row 53 and foll 5 alt rows:** Purl.
**Row 54:** *K13, (k2tog) twice, k13; rep from * once (56 sts).
**Row 56:** *K12, (k2tog) twice, k12; rep from * once (52 sts).
**Row 58:** *K11, (k2tog) twice, k11; rep from * once (48 sts).
**Row 60:** *K10, (k2tog) twice, k10; rep from * once (44 sts).
**Row 62:** *K9, (k2tog) twice, k9; rep from * once (40 sts).
**Row 64:** *K8, (k2tog) twice, k8; rep from * once (36 sts).
Cast off pwise.

## Head
Using the long tail method and yarn A, cast on 8 sts.

**Row 1 and foll 4 alt rows:** Purl.
**Row 2:** (Kfb) to end (16 sts).
**Row 4:** (Kfb, k1) to end (24 sts).
**Row 6:** (Kfb, k2) to end (32 sts).
**Row 8:** (Kfb, k3) to end (40 sts).
**Row 10:** (Kfb, k4) to end (48 sts).
**Rows 11 to 31:** Work 21 rows in st-st.
**Row 32:** (K2tog, k4) to end (40 sts).
**Row 33 and foll 3 alt rows:** Purl.
**Row 34:** (K2tog, k3) to end (32 sts).
**Row 36:** (K2tog, k2) to end (24 sts).
**Row 38:** (K2tog, k1) to end (16 sts).
**Row 40:** (K2tog) to end (8 sts).
Break yarn and thread through sts on needle, pull tight and secure by threading yarn a second time through sts.

## Snout
Using the long tail method and yarn A, cast on 40 sts.

**Rows 1 to 9:** Beg with a p row, work 9 rows in st-st.
**Row 10:** *K4, (k2tog) twice, k4, (k2tog) twice, k4; rep from * once (32 sts).
**Row 11 and foll alt row:** Purl.
**Row 12:** *K3, (k2tog) twice, k2, (k2tog) twice, k3; rep from * once (24 sts).
**Row 14:** *K2, (k2tog) 4 times, k2; rep from * once (16 sts).
Cast off pwise.

## Pouch
Using the long tail method and yarn A, cast on 20 sts.

**Row 1:** Purl.
**Row 2:** K1, (m1, k2) to last st, m1, k1 (30 sts).
**Rows 3 to 5:** Work 3 rows in st-st.
**Row 6:** K2, (m1, k2) to end (44 sts).
**Rows 7 to 27:** Work 21 rows in st-st.
**Rows 28 and 29:** Work 2 rows in g-st.
**Rows 30 and 31:** K 1 row then p 1 row.
Cast off.

## Hind legs (make 2)
Using the long tail method and yarn A, cast on 28 sts.

**Row 1:** Purl.
**Row 2:** K4, (m1, k2) 4 times, k6, (m1, k2) 4 times, k2 (36 sts).
**Rows 3 to 21:** Work 19 rows in st-st.
**Row 22:** K6, (k2tog, k2) twice, k10, (k2tog, k2) twice, k4 (32 sts).
**Row 23 and foll alt row:** Purl.
**Row 24:** K5, (k2tog, k2) twice, k8, (k2tog, k2) twice, k3 (28 sts).
**Row 26:** K4, (k2tog, k2) twice, k6, (k2tog, k2) twice, k2 (24 sts).
Cast off pwise.

## Feet (make 2)

Using the long tail method and yarn A, cast on 10 sts.

**Row 1:** Purl.
**Row 2:** (Kfb) to end (20 sts).
**Rows 3 to 21:** Beg with a p row, work 19 rows in st-st.
**Row 22:** (K2tog) to end (10 sts).
Break yarn and thread through sts on needle, pull tight and secure by threading yarn a second time through sts.

## Tail

Using the long tail method and yarn A, cast on 18 sts.

**Row 1:** Purl.
**Row 2:** K4, (m1, k2) twice, k4, (m1, k2) twice, k2 (22 sts).
**Rows 3 to 17:** Work 15 rows in st-st.
**Row 18:** K2tog, k6, w1 (see special abbreviation), turn.
**Row 19:** S1p, p to end (21 sts).
**Row 20:** Knit.
**Row 21:** P2tog, p6, w1, turn.
**Row 22:** S1k, k to end (20 sts).
**Row 23:** Purl.
**Row 24:** K2tog, k5, w1, turn.
**Row 25:** S1p, p to end (19 sts).
**Row 26:** Knit.
**Row 27:** P2tog, p5, w1, turn.
**Row 28:** S1k, k to end (18 sts).
**Row 29:** Purl.
**Row 30:** K2tog, k4, w1, turn.
**Row 31:** S1p, p to end (17 sts).
**Row 32:** Knit.
**Row 33:** P2tog, p4, w1, turn.
**Row 34:** S1k, k to end (16 sts).
**Row 35:** Purl.
**Row 36:** K2tog, k3, w1, turn.
**Row 37:** S1p, p to end (15 sts).
**Row 38:** Knit.
**Row 39:** P2tog, p3, w1, turn.
**Row 40:** S1k, k to end (14 sts).
**Row 41 and foll alt row:** Purl.

**Row 42:** K2tog, k to last 2 sts, k2tog (12 sts).
**Row 44:** (K2tog) to end (6 sts).
Break yarn and thread through sts on needle, pull tight and secure by threading yarn a second time through sts.

## Forearms (make 2)

Using the long tail method and yarn A, cast on 6 sts.

**Row 1 and foll 2 alt rows:** Purl.
**Row 2:** K1, m1, k4, m1, k1 (8 sts).
**Row 4:** K1, m1, k6, m1, k1 (10 sts).
**Row 6:** K1, m1, k8, m1, k1 (12 sts).
**Rows 7 to 9:** Work 3 rows in st-st.
**Rows 10 and 11:** Cast on 3 sts at the beg of next 2 rows (18 sts).
**Rows 12 to 25:** Work 14 rows in st-st.
**Row 26:** (K2tog) to end (9 sts).
Break yarn and thread through sts on needle, pull tight and secure by threading yarn a second time through sts.

## Ears (make 2)

Using the long tail method and yarn A, cast on 16 sts.

**Rows 1 to 3:** Beg with a p row, work 3 rows in st-st.
**Row 4:** K3, (m1, k2) twice, k4, (m1, k2) twice, k1 (20 sts).
**Rows 5 to 7:** Work 3 rows in st-st.
**Row 8:** K7, k2tog tbl, k2, k2tog, k7 (18 sts).
**Row 9 and foll 3 alt rows:** Purl.
**Row 10:** K6, k2tog tbl, k2, k2tog, k6 (16 sts).
**Row 12:** K5, k2tog tbl, k2, k2tog, k5 (14 sts).
**Row 14:** K4, k2tog tbl, k2, k2tog, k4 (12 sts).
**Row 16:** (K2tog) to end (6 sts).
**Row 17:** Purl.
Break yarn and thread through sts on needle, pull tight and secure by threading yarn a second time through sts.

# Making up Kangaroo

**Note:** Sew up all row-end seams on right side using mattress stitch one stitch in from the edge, unless otherwise stated; a one-stitch seam allowance has been allowed for this.

## Body and head and snout
Gather round cast-on stitches of body, pull tight and secure. Sew up side edges of body and stuff. Sew up side edges of head leaving a gap, stuff and sew up gap. Pin and sew head to neck of body taking a horizontal stitch from head then a horizontal stitch from body and do this alternately all the way round. Sew up side edges of muzzle, stuff, pin to head and sew muzzle to head.

## Pouch
Fold over top edge of pouch along garter stitch row and sew cast-off stitches in place. Pin and sew side edges of pouch to marking lines on body and sew across lower edge.

## Hind legs and feet
Sew up side edges of hind legs and with this seam at centre of inside edge, sew across top. Stuff and sew across lower edge. Sew hind legs to Kangaroo at both sides. Sew up side edges of feet, stuff, and with seam at centre of underneath sew across cast-on stitches. Sew feet to hind legs.

## Tail
Sew up side edges of tail, stuffing tail as you sew. With the seam at centre of underneath, sew across cast-on stitches. Sew tail to Kangaroo.

## Forearms
Sew up side edges of forearms from paw to cast-off stitches at underarm. Stuff forearms and sew to sides of Kangaroo.

## Ears
Sew up side edges of ears, fold lower edge in half and sew ears to head.

## Features
Using picture as a guide, mark position of eyes with two pins and embroider eyes in black making a vertical chain stitch for each eye, then a second chain stitch on top of first. Embroider nose in satin stitch and mouth in straight stitches (see page 163 for how to begin and fasten off invisibly for the embroidery).

# How to make Joey

## Body
Using the long tail method and yarn A, cast on 16 sts.
**Row 1 and foll alt row:** Purl.
**Row 2:** K2, (kfb) 4 times, k4, (kfb) 4 times, k2 (24 sts).
**Row 4:** K5, (kfb) twice, k10, (kfb) twice, k5 (28 sts).
**Rows 5 to 9:** Work 5 rows in st-st.
**Row 10:** K3, (k2tog) 4 times, k6, (k2tog) 4 times, k3 (20 sts).
**Rows 11 to 17:** Work 7 rows in st-st.
**Row 18:** K1, (k2tog, k2) to last 3 sts, k2tog, k1 (15 sts).
**Row 19:** Purl.
Cast off.

## Head
Using the long tail method and yarn A, cast on 8 sts.
**Row 1 and foll alt row:** Purl.
**Row 2:** (Kfb) to end (16 sts).
**Row 4:** (Kfb, k1) to end (24 sts).
**Rows 5 to 10:** Work 6 rows in st-st ending with a k row.
**Row 11:** (P2tog, p1) to end (16 sts).
**Row 12:** (K1 tbl) to end.
**Rows 13 to 15:** Work 3 rows in st-st.
**Row 16:** (K2tog) to end (8 sts).
Break yarn and thread through sts on needle, pull tight and secure by threading yarn a second time through sts.

## Hind legs (make 2)
Using the long tail method and yarn A, cast on 12 sts.
**Rows 1 to 7:** Beg with a p row, work 7 rows in st-st.
Break yarn, thread through sts on needle and leave loose.

## Tail

Using the long tail method and yarn A, cast on 12 sts.

**Rows 1 to 9:** Beg with a p row, work 9 rows in st-st.

**Row 10:** (K2tog) to end (6 sts). Break yarn, thread through sts on needle and leave loose.

## Forearms (make 2)

Using the long tail method and yarn A, cast on 12 sts.

**Rows 1 to 5:** Beg with a p row, work 5 rows in st-st. Break yarn, thread through sts on needle and leave loose.

## Ears (make 2)

Using the long tail method and yarn A, cast on 8 sts.

**Rows 1 to 3:** Beg with a p row, work 3 rows in st-st.

**Row 4:** (K2tog) to end (4 sts).

**Row 5:** Purl. Break yarn and thread through sts on needle, pull tight and secure by threading yarn a second time through sts.

# Making up Joey

**Note:** Sew up all row-end seams on right side using mattress stitch one stitch in from the edge, unless otherwise stated; a one-stitch seam allowance has been allowed for this.

## Body and head

Sew up side edges of body and with this seam at centre back, sew across cast-on stitches. Stuff body. Gather round cast-on stitches of head, pull tight and secure. Sew up side edges of head leaving a gap, stuff and sew up gap. Sew head to neck of body.

## Hind legs

Roll up hind legs from row ends to row ends and sew outside edge down. Pull stitches on a thread tight and fasten off and gather round cast-on stitches, pull tight and secure. Sew legs to sides of body.

## Tail

Roll up tail from row ends to row ends and sew outside edge down. Pull stitches on a thread tight and fasten off. Sew cast-on stitches to back of Joey.

## Forearms

Roll up forearms from row ends to row ends and sew outside edge down. Pull stitches on a thread tight and fasten off. Sew forearms to body.

## Ears

Sew up side edges of ears and sew ears to head.

## Features

Using picture as a guide, mark position of eyes with two pins and embroider eyes in black making a vertical chain stitch for each eye. Embroider nose in satin stitch and mouth in straight stitches (see page 163 for how to begin and fasten off invisibly for the embroidery).

# Llama

# Information you'll need

## Materials
Any DK (US: light worsted) yarn
(amounts given are approximate)
**Yarn A** dark cream (50g)
**Yarn B** black (5g)
**Yarn C** white (5g)
**Yarn D** orange (5g)
**Yarn E** yellow (5g)
**Yarn F** purple (5g)
**Yarn G** green (5g)
Oddment of black for embroidery and orange, purple
and green for making up
1 pair of 3.25mm (UK10:US3) needles
Knitters' pins and a blunt-ended needle for sewing up
Tweezers (optional)
Acrylic toy stuffing

## Finished size
Llama measures 11in (28cm) high

## Tension
26 sts x 34 rows measure 4in (10cm) square over st-st
using 3.25mm needles and DK yarn before stuffing, or
needles to give correct tension.

## Abbreviations
See page 164

# How to make Llama

### Body, neck and head

Using the long tail method and yarn A, cast on 28 sts and work in moss-st.

**Row 1:** (P1, k1) to end (this row sets moss-st).

**Row 2:** *K1, p1, (kfb) twice, (k1, p1) 3 times (kfb) twice, k1, p1; rep from * once (36 sts).

**Row 3:** As row 1.

**Row 4:** *K1, p1, (kfb) twice, (k1, p1) 5 times (kfb) twice, k1, p1; rep from * once (44 sts).

**Row 5:** As row 1.

**Row 6:** *(K1, p1) twice, (kfb) twice, (k1, p1) 5 times (kfb) twice, (k1, p1) twice; rep from * once (52 sts).

**Row 7:** As row 1.

**Row 8:** *(K1, p1) twice, (kfb) twice, (k1, p1) 7 times (kfb) twice, (k1, p1) twice; rep from * once (60 sts).

**Rows 9 to 31:** Work 23 rows in moss-st.

**Row 32:** (K1, p1) twice, p3tog tbl, (p1, k1) 23 times, p3tog, (k1, p1) twice (56 sts).

**Row 33:** As row 1.

**Row 34:** (K1, p1) twice, p3tog tbl, (p1, k1) 21 times, p3tog, (k1, p1) twice (52 sts).

**Row 35:** As row 1.

**Row 36:** (P3tog tbl, p1) twice, (k1, p1) 18 times, (k1, p3tog) twice (44 sts).

**Row 37:** Beg with a p st, cast off 10 sts in moss-st, (k1, p1) 11 times, k1, cast off rem 10 sts in moss-st and fasten off.

**Row 38:** Rejoin yarn to rem sts and (k1, p1) to end (24 sts).

**Rows 39 to 69:** Work 31 rows in moss-st.

**Row 70:** *(P2tog) twice, k1, p1; rep from * 4 times (16 sts).

**Row 71:** (P1, k1) to end.

**Row 72:** (K1, p1) to end.

**Row 73:** (K2tog, p1, k1) to end (12 sts).
Break yarn and thread through sts on needle, pull tight and secure by threading yarn a second time through sts.

### Legs (make 4)

Using the long tail method and yarn B, cast on 7 sts.

**Row 1 and foll alt row:** Purl.

**Row 2:** K1, (kfb) twice, k1, (kfb) twice, k1 (11 sts).

**Row 4:** K2, (kfb, k1) 4 times, k1 (15 sts).

**Rows 5 to 7:** Beg with a p row, work 3 rows in st-st.

**Row 8:** K3, (k2tog) twice, k1, (k2tog) twice, k3 (11 sts).

**Rows 9 to 23:** Change to yarn C and beg with a p row, work 15 rows in st-st.

**Row 24:** Change to yarn A and k 1 row.

**Row 25:** K2, (m1, k1) to last st, k1 (19 sts).

**Row 26:** K1, (p1, k1) to end.

**Rows 27 to 45:** Rep row 26, 19 times more.
Cast off in moss-st.

### Snout

Using the long tail method and yarn C, cast on 18 sts.

**Rows 1 to 5:** Beg with a p row, work 5 rows in st-st.

**Row 6:** (K2tog) to end (9 sts).
Break yarn and thread through sts on needle, pull tight and secure by threading yarn a second time through sts.

### Ears (make 2)

Using the long tail method and yarn C, cast on 5 sts.

**Row 1:** Purl.

**Row 2:** K1, (m1, k1) to end (9 sts).

**Rows 3 to 5:** Beg with a p row, work 3 rows in st-st.

**Row 6:** K2, k2tog, k1, k2tog, k2 to end (7 sts).

**Rows 7 and 8:** P 1 row then k 1 row.

**Row 9:** P1, (p2tog, p1) twice (5 sts).

**Row 10:** Knit.
Break yarn and thread through sts on needle, pull tight and secure by threading yarn a second time through sts.

work in stripes, carrying yarn loosely up side of work.

**Rows 3 and 4:** Yarn E-work 2 rows in g-st.
**Rows 5 and 6:** Yarn F-work 2 rows in g-st.
**Rows 7 and 8:** Yarn G-work 2 rows in g-st.
**Rows 9 to 26:** Rep rows 3 to 8, 3 times more.
**Rows 27 to 29:** Cont in yarn D-work 3 rows in g-st.
Cast off in g-st.

**Borders**
Using yarn D, pick up and knit 16 sts from row ends.
**Rows 1 and 2:** Work 2 rows in g-st.
Cast off in g-st.

## Making up Llama

**Note:** Sew up all row-end seams on right side using mattress stitch one stitch in from the edge, unless otherwise stated; a one-stitch seam allowance has been allowed for this.

### Body, neck and head
Oversew side edges and across back. Stuff neck and body, fold cast-on stitches in half and oversew.

### Legs
Gather round cast-on stitches of legs and sew up side edges of feet. Place a small ball of stuffing into feet. Sew up side edges of legs and stuff, pushing stuffing into narrow part with tweezers or tip of scissors.

### Snout
Sew up side edges of snout and stuff snout. Pin and sew snout to front of head.

### Ears
Fold ears lengthways with wrong sides together and oversew side edges. Sew ears to head at each side.

### Tail
Oversew side edges of tail and stuff. Pin and sew tail to back of Llama.

### Features
Using picture as a guide, mark position of eyes with two pins and embroider eyes in black making a chain stitch for each eye, then a second chain stitch on top of first. Using straight stitches, embroider two eyelashes and a 'y' shape for mouth (see page 163 for how to begin and fasten off invisibly for the embroidery).

### Blanket
Place blanket on Llama and sew down lower edges of blanket. Make a twisted cord from orange yarn starting with the yarn 48in (120cm) in length. Tie middle of twisted cord to blanket at back of neck, then tie twisted cord around neck of Llama with a bow. Knot ends 1½in (4cm) from bow and trim ends. Make four tassels, two in purple and two in green, by winding yarn ten times round two fingers. Cut through all strands and lay in a bundle. Tie middle of bundle tightly with matching yarn and fold bundle in half, keeping one strand of yarn just used to tie for sewing on tassel. Tie a tight yarn around tassel ¼in (6mm) below fold and run ends into centre of tassel. Trim ends of tassels to ½in (13mm). Attach tassels to four corners of blanket.

### Tail
Using the long tail method and yarn C, cast on 20 sts and work in moss-st.
**Row 1:** (K1, p1) to end.
**Row 2:** (P1, k1) to end.
**Rows 3 to 8:** Rep rows 1 and 2, 3 times more.
**Row 9:** (K2tog, k1, p1) to end (15 sts).
Break yarn and thread through sts on needle, pull tight and secure by threading yarn a second time through sts.

### Blanket
Using the long tail method and yarn D, cast on 30 sts and work in g-st.
**Rows 1 and 2:** Work 2 rows in g-st.
Join on yarn E, F and G as needed and

# Fox

# Information you'll need

## Materials
Any DK (US: light worsted) yarn
(amounts given are approximate)
**Yarn A** ginger (40g)
**Yarn B** white (20g) (2 separate balls needed
for intarsia)
**Yarn C** black (20g)
Oddment of black for embroidery
1 pair of 3.25mm (UK10:US3) needles
Knitters' pins and a blunt-ended needle for sewing up
Acrylic toy stuffing

## Finished size
Fox measures 7½in (19cm) tall

## Tension
26 sts x 34 rows measure 4in (10cm) square over
st-st using 3.25mm needles and DK yarn before
stuffing, or needles to give correct tension.

## Abbreviations
See page 164

# How to make Fox

## Body

Using the long tail method and yarn A, cast on 28 sts.

**Row 1 and foll 2 alt rows:** Purl.
**Row 2:** *(K2, m1) twice, k6, (m1, k2) twice; rep from * once (36 sts).
**Row 4:** *(K2, m1) twice, k10, (m1, k2) twice; rep from * once (44 sts).
**Row 6:** *(K2, m1) twice, k14, (m1, k2) twice; rep from * once (52 sts).
**Rows 7 to 33:** Work 27 rows in st-st.
**Row 34:** K23, cast off next 6 sts, k to end (46 sts).
**Row 35:** P23, turn and work on these 23 sts.
**Row 36:** K2tog, k to end (22 sts).
**Row 37:** Purl.
**Rows 38 to 41:** Rep rows 36 and 37 twice more (20 sts).
**Rows 42 to 45:** Change to yarn B and rep rows 36 and 37 twice more (18 sts).
**Row 46:** K12, (k2tog, k1) twice (16 sts).
**Row 47 and foll alt row:** Purl.
**Row 48:** K10, (k2tog, k1) twice (14 sts).
**Row 50:** K8, (k2tog, k1) twice (12 sts).
**Row 51:** Purl.
Cast off.
**Row 52:** Rejoin yarn A to rem sts and p 1 row (23 sts).
**Row 53:** K to last 2 sts, k2tog (22 sts).
**Row 54:** Purl.
**Rows 55 to 58:** Rep rows 53 and 54 twice more (20 sts).
**Rows 59 to 62:** Change to yarn B and rep rows 53 and 54 twice more (18 sts).
**Row 63:** (K1, k2tog) twice, k to end (16 sts).
**Row 64:** Purl.
**Rows 65 to 68:** Rep rows 63 and 64 twice more (12 sts).
Cast off.

## Head

Using the long tail method and yarn C, cast on 6 sts.
**Row 1:** (Kfb) to end (12 sts).
**Row 2:** Purl.
**Row 3:** Knit.
Break off yarn C and join on yarn A and 2 balls of yarn B and work in intarsia in blocks of colours, twisting yarn when changing colours to avoid a hole.
**Row 4:** Yarn B-k4, yarn A-k4, yarn B (second ball)-k4.
**Row 5:** Yarn B-p4, yarn A-p4, yarn B-p4.
**Row 6:** Yarn B-*k1, m1, k2, m1, k1,** yarn A-rep from * to ** once, yarn B-rep from * to ** once (18 sts).
**Row 7:** Yarn B-p6, yarn A-p6, yarn B-p6.
**Row 8:** Yarn B-*k1, m1, k4, m1, k1,** yarn A-k6, yarn B-rep from * to ** once (22 sts).
**Row 9:** Yarn B-p8, yarn A-p6, yarn B-p8.
**Row 10:** Yarn B-*k1, m1, k6, m1, k1,** yarn A-k6, yarn B-rep from * to ** once (26 sts).

**Row 11:** Yarn B-p10, yarn A-p6, yarn B-p10.
**Row 12:** Yarn B-*k1, m1, k8, m1, k1,** yarn A-k1, m1, k4, m1, k1, yarn B-rep from * to ** once (32 sts).
**Row 13:** Yarn B-p12, yarn A-p8, yarn B-p12.
**Row 14:** Yarn B-*k1, m1, k10, m1, k1,** yarn A-k8, yarn B-rep from * to ** once (36 sts).
**Row 15:** Yarn B-p14, yarn A-p8, yarn B-p14.
**Row 16:** Yarn B-k14, yarn A-k8, yarn B-k14.
**Row 17:** As row 15.
**Row 18:** Yarn B-k8, yarn A (rejoin yarn A)-k20, yarn B (rejoin yarn B)-k8.
**Row 19:** Yarn B-p8, yarn A-p20, yarn B-p8.
**Row 20:** Yarn B-k7, yarn A-(m1, k2) 11 times, m1, yarn B-k7 (48 sts).
**Row 21:** Yarn B-p7, yarn A-p34, yarn B-p7.
**Row 22:** Yarn B-k6, yarn A-k36, yarn B-k6.
**Row 23:** Yarn B-p6, yarn A-p36, yarn B-p6.
**Row 24:** Yarn B-k5, yarn A-k38, yarn B-k5.
**Row 25:** Yarn B-p5, yarn A-p38, yarn B-p5.
**Row 26:** Yarn B-k4, yarn A-k40, yarn B-k4.
**Row 27:** Yarn B-p4, yarn A-p40, yarn B-p4.
**Rows 28 to 33:** Rejoin yarn A and cont in yarn A, work 6 rows in st-st.
**Row 34:** (K2tog, k4) to end (40 sts).
**Row 35 and foll 3 alt rows:** Purl.
**Row 36:** (K2tog, k3) to end (32 sts).
**Row 38:** (K2tog, k2) to end (24 sts).
**Row 40:** (K2tog, k1) to end (16 sts).
**Row 42:** (K2tog) to end (8 sts).
Break yarn and thread through sts on needle, pull tight and secure by threading yarn a second time through sts.

## Legs (make 4)

Using the long tail method and yarn C, cast on 10 sts.
**Row 1:** Purl.
**Row 2:** (Kfb) to end (20 sts).
**Rows 3 to 7:** Beg with a p row, work 5 rows in st-st.
**Row 8:** K4, (k2tog) 6 times, k4 (14 sts).
**Rows 9 to 17:** Work 9 rows in st-st.

**Rows 18 to 27:** Change to yarn A and work 10 rows in st-st.
**Row 28:** K1, (k2tog, k3) twice, k2tog, k1 (11 sts).
**Row 29:** Purl.
Cast off.

## Ears (make 2)
Using the long tail method and yarn A, cast on 14 sts.
**Rows 1 to 3:** Beg with a p row, work 3 rows in st-st.
**Row 4:** K4, k2tog, k2, k2tog, k4 (12 sts).
**Rows 5 to 7:** Work 3 rows in st-st.
**Row 8:** (K2tog) to end (6 sts).
Break yarn and thread through sts on needle, pull tight and secure by threading yarn a second time through sts.

## Ear linings (make 2)
Using the long tail method and yarn B, cast on 8 sts.
**Rows 1 to 3:** Beg with a p row, work 3 rows in st-st.
**Row 4:** K3, k2tog, k3 (7 sts).
**Row 5:** Purl.
**Row 6:** K1, (k2tog, k1) twice (5 sts).
**Row 7:** P1, p3tog, p1 (3 sts).
Break yarn and thread through sts on needle, pull tight and secure by threading yarn a second time through sts.

## Tail
Using the long tail method and yarn A, cast on 9 sts.
**Rows 1 to 7:** Beg with a p row, work 7 rows in st-st.
**Row 8:** K1, (m1, k2) to end (13 sts).
**Rows 9 to 13:** Work 5 rows in st-st.
**Row 14:** K1, (m1, k3) to end (17 sts).
**Rows 15 to 19:** Work 5 rows in st-st.
**Row 20:** K1, (m1, k4) to end (21 sts).
**Rows 21 to 25:** Work 5 rows in st-st.
**Row 26:** K1, (m1, k5) to end (25 sts).

**Rows 27 to 31:** Work 5 rows in st-st.
**Rows 32 to 39:** Change to yarn B and work 8 rows in st-st.
**Row 40:** (K2tog, k3) to end (20 sts).
**Row 41 and foll 2 alt rows:** Purl.
**Row 42:** (K2tog, k2) to end (15 sts).
**Row 44:** (K2tog, k1) to end (10 sts).
**Row 46:** (K2tog) to end (5 sts).
Break yarn and thread through sts on needle, pull tight and secure by threading yarn a second time through sts.

# Making up Fox

**Note:** Sew up all row-end seams on right side using mattress stitch one stitch in from the edge, unless otherwise stated; a one-stitch seam allowance has been allowed for this.

## Body
Fold cast-on stitches in half and sew together. Sew up side edges and cast-off stitches leaving neck open. Stuff body.

## Head
Weave in ends around intarsia. Gather round cast-on stitches, pull tight and secure. Sew up side edges leaving a gap, stuff head pushing stuffing into nose and sew up gap. Sew head to neck of body all the way round.

## Legs
Fold cast-on stitches in half and sew up, then fold cast-off stitches in half and sew up. Sew up side edges of foot and place a small ball of stuffing into foot. Sew up remaining side edges leaving a gap, stuff and sew up gap. Sew legs to body.

## Ears
Sew up side edges of tips of ears and place wrong sides of one ear and one

ear lining together. Sew in place. Repeat for other ear and sew ears to head.

## Tail
Sew up side edges of tail, stuffing as you sew. Sew tail to Fox.

## Features
Using picture as a guide, mark position of eyes with two pins and embroider eyes in black making a vertical chain stitch for each eye, then a second chain stitch on top of first (see page 163 for how to begin and fasten off invisibly for the embroidery).

# Sloth

# Information you'll need

## Materials
Any DK (US: light worsted) yarn
(amounts given are approximate)
**Yarn A** brown (50g)
**Yarn B** cream (10g)
**Yarn C** dark brown (5g)
Oddment of black for embroidery
1 pair of 3.25mm (UK10:US3) needles
Knitters' pins and a blunt-ended needle for sewing up
Acrylic toy stuffing

## Finished size
Sloth measures 8in (20.5cm) long

## Tension
26 sts x 34 rows measure 4in (10cm)
square over st-st using 3.25mm
needles and DK yarn before stuffing,
or needles to give correct tension.

## Abbreviations
See page 164

**Row 26:** K30, (kfb, k2) 4 times, k28 (74 sts).
**Rows 27 to 38:** Work 12 rows in g-st.
**Row 39:** (K2, k2tog) twice, k22, (k2tog, k2) 4 times, k20, (k2tog, k2) twice (66 sts).
**Rows 40 to 42:** Work 3 row in g-st.
**Row 43:** (K2, k2tog) twice, k18, (k2tog, k2) 4 times, k16, (k2tog, k2) twice (58 sts).
**Row 44:** Knit.
**Row 45:** (K2, k2tog) twice, k14, (k2tog, k2) 4 times, k12, (k2tog, k2) twice (50 sts).
**Rows 46 to 51:** Work 6 rows in g-st.
**Row 52:** (K2, kfb) twice, k14, (kfb, k2) 4 times, k12, (kfb, k2) twice (58 sts).
**Row 53:** Knit.
**Row 54:** (K2, kfb) twice, k18, (kfb, k2) 4 times, k16, (kfb, k2) twice (66 sts).
**Rows 55 to 66:** Work 12 rows in g-st.
**Row 67:** (K2, k2tog) twice, k17, (k2tog, k2) twice, (k2, k2tog) twice, k17, (k2tog, k2) twice (58 sts).
**Rows 68 to 70:** Work 3 rows in g-st.
**Row 71:** (K2, k2tog) twice, k13, (k2tog, k2) twice, (k2, k2tog) twice, k13, (k2tog, k2) twice (50 sts).
**Row 72:** Knit.
**Row 73:** (K2, k2tog) twice, k9, (k2tog, k2) twice, (k2, k2tog) twice, k9, (k2tog, k2) twice (42 sts).
**Row 74:** Knit.
**Row 75:** (K2, k2tog) twice, k5, (k2tog) twice, k4, (k2tog) twice, k5, (k2tog, k2) twice (34 sts).
**Row 76:** Knit.
**Row 77:** K2, (k2tog) twice, k5, (k2tog) twice, k4, (k2tog) twice, k5, (k2tog) twice, k2 (26 sts).
Cast off in g-st.

## How to make Sloth

### Body and head
Using the long tail method and yarn A, cast on 34 sts and work in g-st.
**Row 1:** Knit.
**Row 2:** (K2, kfb) twice, k6, (kfb, k2) 4 times, k4, (kfb, k2) twice (42 sts).
**Rows 3 to 5:** Work 3 rows in g-st.
**Row 6:** (K2, kfb) twice, k10, (kfb, k2) 4 times, k8, (kfb, k2) twice (50 sts).
**Rows 7 to 9:** Work 3 rows in g-st.
**Row 10:** (K2, kfb) twice, k14, (kfb, k2) 4 times, k12, (kfb, k2) twice (58 sts).
**Rows 11 to 13:** Work 3 rows in g-st.
**Row 14:** K24, (kfb, k2) 4 times, k22 (62 sts).
**Rows 15 to 17:** Work 3 rows in g-st.
**Row 18:** K26, (kfb, k2) 4 times, k24 (66 sts).
**Rows 19 to 21:** Work 3 rows in g-st.
**Row 22:** K28, (kfb, k2) 4 times, k26 (70 sts).
**Rows 23 to 25:** Work 3 rows in g-st.

### Face piece
Using the long tail method and yarn B, cast on 60 sts.
**Rows 1 and 2:** P 2 rows.
**Row 3:** K9, (k2tog) 6 times, k18, (k2tog) 6 times, k9 (48 sts).
**Row 4 and foll 3 alt rows:** Purl.
**Row 5:** K8, (k2tog) 4 times, k16, (k2tog) 4 times, k8 (40 sts).
**Row 7:** K6, (k2tog) 4 times, k12, (k2tog) 4 times, k6 (32 sts).
**Row 9:** K2, (k2tog) 6 times, k4, (k2tog) 6 times, k2 (20 sts).
**Row 11:** (K2tog) to end (10 sts).
Break yarn and thread through sts on needle, pull tight and secure by threading yarn a second time through sts.

### Forearms (make 2)
Using the long tail method and yarn A, cast on 18 sts and beg in g-st.
**Row 1:** Knit.
**Row 2:** (K1, kfb, k5, kfb, k1) twice (22 sts).
**Rows 3 to 18:** Work 16 rows in g-st.
**Row 19:** K8, k2tog, k2, k2tog, k8 (20 sts).
**Row 20:** Knit.
**Row 21:** K7, k2tog, k2, k2tog, k7 (18 sts).**
**Rows 22 to 46:** Work 25 rows in g-st.
***Row 47:** K2, (k2tog) 3 times, k2, (k2tog) 3 times, k2 (12 sts).
Sl 4 sts pwise at beg of row from LH needle to RH needle.
**Row 48:** Join on yarn B to halfway along row, p4, turn.
**Row 49:** K1, (m1, k1) 3 times (7 sts).
Turn and work on these 7 sts.
**Rows 50 to 56:** Beg with a p row, work 7 rows in st-st.
Break yarn and thread through sts, pull tight and secure by threading yarn a second time through sts. Sew up side edges of toe using mattress stitch from tip to base leaving ends on wrong side.

**Row 57:** With WS facing, slip 2 sts from RH needle to LH needle, rejoin yarn B, p4, turn.
**Rows 58 to 74:** Rep rows 49 to 57 once then rows 49 to 56 once.
Break yarn and thread through sts, pull tight and secure by threading yarn a second time through sts. Sew up side edges of toe using mattress stitch from tip to base.

## Hind legs (make 2)
Using the long tail method and yarn A, cast on 18 sts and beg in g-st.
**Rows 1 to 21:** Work from beg to **, as for forearms.
**Rows 22 to 36:** Work 15 rows in g-st.
**Rows 37 to 64:** Rep from *** to end, as for forearms.

## Nose
Using the long tail method and yarn C, cast on 5 sts.
**Row 1:** Purl.
**Row 2:** K1, m1, k3, m1, k1 (7 sts).
**Rows 3 to 5:** Work 3 rows in st-st.

**Row 6:** K2tog, k3, k2tog (5 sts).
Cast off pwise.

## Eye patches (make 2)
Using the long tail method and yarn C, cast on 5 sts.
**Row 1:** Purl.
**Row 2:** K1, m1, k to last st, m1, k1 (7 sts).
**Rows 3 and 4:** Rep rows 1 and 2 once (9 sts).
**Rows 5 to 11:** Work 7 rows in st-st.
**Row 12:** K2tog, k to last 2 sts, k2tog (7 sts).
**Row 13:** Purl.
**Row 14:** K2tog, k to last 2 sts, k2tog (5 sts).
Cast off pwise.

## Making up Sloth

**Note:** Sew up all row-end seams on right side using mattress stitch one stitch in from the edge, unless otherwise stated; a one-stitch seam allowance has been allowed for this.

### Body and head
Fold cast-on stitches in half and oversew. Fold cast-off stitches in half and oversew. Sew up side edges of body leaving a gap, stuff head and body and sew up gap.

### Face piece, eye patches and features
Using picture as a guide, sew face piece to one side of head and nose to centre of face. Pin and sew eye patches to face. Mark position of eyes with two pins and embroider eyes in black making a vertical chain stitch for each eye, then a second chain stitch on top of first. Embroider mouth in stem stitch using black making a curved line below snout (see page 163 for how to begin and fasten off invisibly for the embroidery).

### Forearms and hind legs
Sew base of toes between toes together on wrong side. Oversew side edges of forearms and hind legs and stuff. Fold cast-on edges in half and oversew. Pin and sew cast-on stitches of arms and legs to Sloth, positioning shoulders of forearms behind hind legs with toes level.

# Swan with Cygnets

# Information you'll need

## Materials

Any DK (US: light worsted) yarn
(amounts given are approximate)
**Yarn A** white (130g)
**Yarn B** black (5g)
**Yarn C** orange (5g)
**Yarn D** dark grey (20g)
**Yarn E** silver grey (70g)
Oddment of black for embroidery
1 pair of 3.25mm (UK10:US3) needles and spare needle
of same size
Knitters' pins and a blunt-ended needle for sewing up
Tweezers (optional)
Acrylic toy stuffing

## Finished size

Swan measures 12in (30.5cm) high
Cygnets measure 3½in (9cm) high

## Tension

26 sts x 34 rows measure 4in (10cm) square over st-st
using 3.25mm needles and DK yarn before stuffing, or
needles to give correct tension.

## Abbreviations

See page 164

## Special abbreviation

**w1** – wrap 1 stitch: take yarn between needles to opposite
side, slip one stitch pwise from LH needle to RH needle
and take yarn back between the needles to first side.

# How to make Swan

## Body, neck and head

### First side

Using the long tail method and yarn A, cast on 34 sts.

**Row 1 and foll 4 alt rows:** Purl.

**Row 2:** (K1, m1) twice, k30, (m1, k1) twice (38 sts).

**Row 4:** (K1, m1) twice, k34, (m1, k1) twice (42 sts).

**Row 6:** (K1, m1) twice, k38, (m1, k1) twice (46 sts).

**Row 8:** (K1, m1) twice, k42, (m1, k1) twice (50 sts).

**Row 10:** (K1, m1) twice, k46, (m1, k1) twice (54 sts).

**Row 11:** Purl.
Break yarn and set aside.

### Second side

**Rows 1 to 11:** Work as first side but do not break yarn.

### Join sides

**Row 12:** K across sts of second side and then with the same yarn cont knitting across sts of first side, then place a marker on first and last st of this row.

**Row 13:** Purl (108 sts).

**Row 14:** (K1, m1) twice, k51, (m1, k2) twice, k49, (m1, k1) twice (114 sts).

**Rows 15 to 17:** Work 3 rows in st-st.

**Row 18:** (K1, m1) twice, k to last 2 sts, (m1, k1) twice (118 sts).

**Rows 19 to 21:** Work 3 rows in st-st.

**Row 22:** As row 18 (122 sts).

**Rows 23 to 35:** Work 13 rows in st-st.

### Shape first side of tail

**Row 36:** K20, w1 (see special abbreviation), turn.

**Row 37:** S1p, p to end.

**Row 38:** K2tog, k16, w1, turn.

**Row 39:** S1p, p to end (121 sts).

**Row 40:** K14, w1, turn.

**Row 41:** S1p, p to end.

**Row 42:** K2tog, k10, w1, turn.

**Row 43:** S1p, p to end (120 sts).

**Row 44:** K8, w1, turn.

**Row 45:** S1p, p to end.

**Row 46:** K2tog, k4, w1, turn.

**Row 47:** S1p, p to end (119 sts).

**Row 48:** K2tog, k2, w1, turn.

**Row 49:** S1p, p to end (118 sts).

**Row 50:** Cast off 37 sts at beg of row, k to end (81 sts).

### Shape second side of tail

**Row 51:** P20, w1, turn.

**Row 52:** S1k, k to end.

**Row 53:** P2tog, p16, w1, turn.

**Row 54:** S1k, k to end (80 sts).

**Row 55:** P14, w1, turn.

**Row 56:** S1k, k to end.

**Row 57:** P2tog, p10, w1, turn.

**Row 58:** S1k, k to end (79 sts).

**Row 59:** P8, w1, turn.

**Row 60:** S1k, k to end.

**Row 61:** P2tog, p4, w1, turn.

**Row 62:** S1k, k to end (78 sts).

**Row 63:** P2tog, p2, w1, turn.

**Row 64:** S1k, k to end (77 sts).

**Row 65:** Cast off 37 sts pwise at beg of row, p to end (40 sts).

**Rows 66 to 73:** Work 8 rows in st-st.

**Row 74:** K1, m1, k to last st, m1, k1 (42 sts).

**Rows 75 to 77:** Work 3 rows in st-st.

**Row 78:** K1, m1, k18, (k2tog) twice, k18, m1, k1.

**Rows 79 to 81:** Work 3 rows in st-st.

**Rows 82 to 93:** Rep rows 78 to 81, 3 times more.

**Row 94:** K19, (k2tog) twice, k19 (40 sts).

**Rows 95 to 97:** Work 3 rows in st-st.

**Row 98:** K18, (k2tog) twice, k18 (38 sts).

**Rows 99 to 101:** Work 3 rows in st-st.

**Row 102:** K17, (k2tog) twice, k17 (36 sts).

**Rows 103 to 105:** Work 3 rows in st-st.

**Row 106:** K14, w1, turn.

**Row 107:** S1p, p to end.

**Row 108:** K10, w1, turn.

**Row 109:** S1p, p to end.

**Row 110:** Knit.

**Row 111:** P14, w1, turn.

**Row 112:** S1k, k to end.

**Row 113:** P10, w1, turn.

**Row 114:** S1k, k to end.

**Row 115:** P2tog, p15, m1, p2, m1, p15, p2tog.

**Rows 116 to 165:** Rep rows 106 to 115, 5 times more.

**Rows 166 and 167:** K 1 row then p 1 row.

**Row 168:** (K2tog, k4) to end (30 sts).

**Row 169 and foll 3 alt rows:** Purl.

**Row 170:** (K2tog, k3) to end (24 sts).

**Row 172:** (K2tog, k2) to end (18 sts).

**Row 174:** (K2tog, k1) to end (12 sts).

**Row 176:** (K2tog) to end (6 sts). Break yarn and thread through sts on needle, pull tight and secure by threading yarn a second time through sts.

## Base
Using the long tail method and yarn A, cast on 3 sts.
**Row 1:** Purl.
**Row 2:** K1, m1, k1, m1, k1 (5 sts).
**Row 3:** Purl.
**Row 4:** K1, m1, k to last st, m1, k1 (7 sts).
**Rows 5 to 22:** Rep rows 3 and 4, 9 times more (25 sts).
**Rows 23 to 57:** Work 35 rows in st-st.
**Row 58:** K2tog, k to last 2 sts, k2tog (23 sts).
**Row 59:** Purl.
**Rows 60 to 77:** Rep rows 58 and 59, 9 times more (5 sts).
**Row 78:** K2tog, k1, k2tog (3 sts).
Break yarn and thread through sts on needle, pull tight and secure by threading yarn a second time through sts.

## Beak
Using the long tail method and yarn B, cast on 43 sts.
**Row 1:** K9, k3tog, k8, k3tog, k8, k3tog, k9 (37 sts).
**Row 2:** K8, k3tog, k2, (m1, k2) twice, k3tog, k2, (m1, k2) twice, k3tog, k8 (35 sts).
Change to yarn C and dec:
**Row 3:** K16, k3tog, k16 (33 sts).
**Row 4 and foll 4 alt rows:** Purl.
**Row 5:** K15, k3tog, k15 (31 sts).
**Row 7:** K14, k3tog, k14 (29 sts).
**Row 9:** K13, k3tog, k13 (27 sts).
**Row 11:** K12, k3tog, k12 (25 sts).
**Row 13:** K2tog, k to last 2 sts, k2tog (23 sts).

**Row 14:** Purl.
**Rows 15 to 24:** Rep rows 13 and 14, 5 times more (13 sts).
**Row 25:** K1, (k2tog, k1) to end (9 sts). Cast off pwise.

## Webbed feet (make 4 pieces)
Using the long tail method and yarn D, cast on 27 sts.
**Row 1:** Purl.
**Row 2:** K2tog, k2, (m1, k2) 4 times, k3tog, k2, (m1, k2) 4 times, k2tog (31 sts).
**Row 3:** P14, p3tog, p14 (29 sts).
**Row 4:** K2tog, k11, k3tog, k11, k2tog (25 sts).
**Row 5 and foll 5 alt rows:** Purl.
**Row 6:** K2tog, k9, k3tog, k9, k2tog (21 sts).
**Row 8:** K2tog, k7, k3tog, k7, k2tog (17 sts).
**Row 10:** K2tog, k5, k3tog, k5, k2tog (13 sts).

**Row 12:** K2tog, k3, k3tog, k3, k2tog (9 sts).
**Row 14:** K2tog, k1, k3tog, k1, k2tog (5 sts).
**Row 16:** K1, k3tog, k1 (3 sts).
Break yarn and thread through sts on needle, pull tight and secure by threading yarn a second time through sts.

## Legs (make 2)
Using the long tail method and yarn D, cast on 10 sts.
**Row 1 and foll 3 alt rows:** Purl.
**Row 2:** K2, m1, k2, m1, k4, k2tog (11 sts).
**Row 4:** K3, m1, k2, m1, k4, k2tog (12 sts).
**Row 6:** K4, m1, k2, m1, k4, k2tog (13 sts).
**Row 8:** K5, m1, k2, m1, k4, k2tog (14 sts).
**Rows 9 to 11:** Work 3 rows in st-st.
**Row 12:** K4, k2tog tbl, k2, k2tog, k3, m1, k1 (13 sts).
**Row 13 and foll 2 alt rows:** Purl.
**Row 14:** K3, k2tog tbl, k2, k2tog, k3, m1, k1 (12 sts).
**Row 16:** K2, k2tog tbl, k2, k2tog, k3, m1, k1 (11 sts).
**Row 18:** K1, k2tog tbl, k2, k2tog, k3, m1, k1 (10 sts).
**Row 19:** Purl.
Cast off.

## Wings
**Right wing**
Using the long tail method and yarn A, cast on 15 sts and beg in g-st.
**Row 1:** Knit.
**Row 2:** K1, m1, k to last st, m1, k1 (17 sts).
**Rows 3 to 20:** Rep rows 1 and 2, 9 times more (35 sts).
**Row 21:** K5, (m1, k5) to end (41 sts).
**Row 22:** K5, (p1, k5) to end.
**Row 23:** K5, (s1p, k5) to end.

**Rows 24 to 55:** Rep rows 22 and 23, 16 times more.
**Row 56:** K5, (p1, k5) 5 times, cast off 6 sts kwise and fasten off (35 sts).
**Row 57:** Rejoin yarn to rem sts and k5, (s1p, k5) to end.
**Row 58:** K5, (p1, k5) to end.
**Row 59:** K5, (s1p, k5) to end.
**Rows 60 to 65:** Rep rows 58 and 59, 3 times more.
**\*\*Row 66:** Cast off 6 sts kwise, k4, (p1, k5) 3 times, cast off rem 6 sts and fasten off (23 sts).
**Row 67:** Rejoin yarn to rem sts and k5, (s1p, k5) to end.
**Row 68:** K5, (p1, k5) to end.
**Row 69:** K5, (s1p, k5) to end.
**Rows 70 to 75:** Rep rows 68 and 69, 3 times more.
**Row 76:** Cast off 6 sts, k4, p1, k5, cast off rem 6 sts and fasten off (11 sts).
**Row 77:** Rejoin yarn to rem sts and k5, s1p, k5.
**Row 78:** K5, p1, k5.
**Row 79:** K5, s1p, k5.
**Rows 80 to 85:** Rep rows 78 and 79, 3 times more.
Cast off.

**Left wing**
Using the long tail method and yarn A, cast on 15 sts and beg in g-st.
**Row 1:** Knit.
**Row 2:** K1, m1, k to last st, m1, k1 (17 sts).
**Rows 3 to 20:** Rep rows 1 and 2, 9 times more (35 sts).

**Row 21:** K5, (m1, k5) to end (41 sts).
**Row 22:** K5, (p1, k5) to end.
**Row 23:** K5, (s1p, k5) to end.
**Rows 24 to 55:** Rep rows 22 and 23, 16 times more.
**Row 56:** Cast off 6 sts kwise k4, (p1, k5) 5 times, (35 sts).
**Row 57:** K5, (s1p, k5) to end.
**Row 58:** K5, (p1, k5) to end.
**Rows 59 to 65:** Rep rows 57 and 58, 3 times more then row 57 once.
**Rows 66 to 85:** Work from \*\* to end, as for right wing.
Cast off.

## Making up Swan

**Note:** Sew up all row-end seams on right side using mattress stitch one stitch in from the edge, unless otherwise stated; a one-stitch seam allowance has been allowed for this.

## Body, neck, head and base
Sew up side edges of head and neck and stuff. Sew across back, around tail and down to markers. Stuff body, pin on base and sew around base keeping base flat.

## Beak and features
Sew up side edges of beak and stuff beak. Pin and sew beak to front of head pointing downwards. Using picture as a guide, embroider eyes in black making a vertical chain stitch for each eye, then two chain stitches on top of first (see page 163 for how to begin and fasten off the embroidery invisibly).

## Legs and webbed feet
Sew up cast-on and cast-off stitches of legs and stuff. Place wrong sides of two pieces of webbed feet together matching all edges and oversew around outside edge. Repeat for second foot and pin and sew straight row ends of legs to feet with legs pointing inwards. Sew shaped edges of both legs to body low down.

## Wings
Oversew top edge of wings together and lightly stuff top of wings. Pin wings to sides of Swan and sew in place.

## How to make Cygnets

### Body
Using the long tail method and yarn E, cast on 20 sts and work in g-st.
**Row 1 and foll 2 alt rows:** Knit.
**Row 2:** *K2, (m1, k2) 4 times; rep from * once (28 sts).
**Row 4:** *(K2, m1) twice, k6, (m1, k2) twice; rep from * once (36 sts).
**Row 6:** *(K2, m1) twice, k10, (m1, k2) twice; rep from * once (44 sts).
**Rows 7 to 26:** Work 20 rows in g-st.
**Row 27:** K15, (k2tog, k2) 4 times, k to end (40 sts).
**Row 28:** Knit.
**Row 29:** K13, (k2tog, k2) 4 times, k to end (36 sts).
**Row 30:** K8, cast off 20 sts (9 sts on RH needle), k to end (16 sts).
**Row 31:** K8, turn and work on these 8 sts.
**Row 32:** K2tog, k6 (7 sts).
**Row 33:** K5, k2tog (6 sts).
**Row 34:** K2tog, k4 (5 sts).
**Row 35:** K3, k2tog (4 sts).
Cast off in g-st.
**Row 36:** Rejoin yarn to rem sts and k to end (8 sts).
**Row 37:** K6, k2tog (7 sts).
**Row 38:** K2tog, k5 (6 sts).
**Row 39:** K4, k2tog (5 sts).
**Row 40:** K2tog, k3 (4 sts).
Cast off in g-st.

### Head
Using the long tail method and yarn E, cast on 24 sts and work in g-st.
**Row 1:** Knit.
**Row 2:** K2, (m1, k4) to last 2 sts, m1, k2 (30 sts).
**Rows 3 to 14:** Work 12 rows in g-st.
**Row 15:** (K2tog, k1) to end (20 sts).
**Row 16 and foll alt row:** Knit.
**Row 17:** (K2tog) to end (10 sts).
**Row 19:** (K2tog) to end (5 sts).

Break yarn and thread through sts on needle, pull tight and secure by threading yarn a second time through sts.

### Beak
Using the long tail method and yarn D, cast on 13 sts.
**Rows 1 to 3:** Beg with a p row, work 3 rows in st-st.
**Row 4:** K2tog, k to last 2 sts, k2tog (11 sts).
**Row 5:** Purl.
**Row 6:** K1, (k2tog) twice, k1, (k2tog) twice, k1 (7 sts).
**Row 7:** Purl.
Break yarn and thread through sts on needle, pull tight and secure by threading yarn a second time through sts.

### Wings (make 2)
Using the long tail method and yarn E, cast on 10 sts and work in g-st.
**Row 1:** Knit.
**Row 2:** K2, (m1, k2) to end (14 sts).
**Rows 3 to 8:** Work 6 rows in g-st.
**Row 9:** K2tog, k to last 2 sts, k2tog (12 sts).
**Row 10:** Knit.
**Rows 11 to 16:** Rep rows 9 and 10, 3 times more (6 sts).
**Row 17:** (K2tog) to end (3 sts).
Break yarn and thread through sts on needle, pull tight and secure by threading yarn a second time through sts.

### Webbed feet (make 2)
Using the long tail method and yarn D, cast on 17 sts.
**Row 1:** Purl.
**Row 2:** K3tog, k4, k3tog, k4, k3tog (11 sts).
**Row 3:** P3tog, p1, p3tog, p1, p3tog (5 sts).
**Row 4:** K1, m1, k3, m1, k1 (7 sts).
**Rows 5 to 7:** Work 3 rows in st-st.
Break yarn and thread through sts on needle, pull tight and secure by threading yarn a second time through sts.

## Making up Cygnets

**Note:** Sew up all row-end seams on right side using mattress stitch one stitch in from the edge, unless otherwise stated; a one-stitch seam allowance has been allowed for this.

### Body
Fold cast-off stitches in half and sew up. Oversew side edges and stuff Cygnet pushing a small ball of stuffing into tail. Fold cast-on stitches in half and oversew.

### Head
Sew up side edges and stuff head. Pin and sew head to body.

### Beak and features
Sew up side edges of beak and stuff beak, pushing stuffing into beak with tweezers or tip of scissors. Using picture as a guide, sew beak to head. Mark position of eyes with two pins and embroider eyes in black making a vertical chain stitch for each eye, then a second chain stitch on top of first (see page 163 for how to begin and fasten off invisibly for the embroidery).

### Wings
Fold wings and sew up side edges and across cast-on stitches. Sew wings to sides leaving tips free.

### Webbed feet
Sew up side edges of feet and with this seam at centre of underneath, sew across cast-on stitches. Sew feet to sides of Cygnet.

# Guinea Pig
# with Pups

# Information you'll need

## Materials
Any DK (US: light worsted) yarn
(amounts given are approximate)
**Yarn A** white (15g)
**Yarn B** charcoal (50g) (2 separate balls
needed for intarsia)
**Yarn C** golden cream (2g)
**Yarn D** dusky pink (5g)
**Yarn E** grey (5g)
Oddment of black for embroidery
1 pair of 3.25mm (UK10:US3) needles
Knitters' pins and a blunt-ended needle
for sewing up
Acrylic toy stuffing

## Finished size
Guinea Pig measures 8in (20.5cm) long
Guinea Pig Pups measure 2¾in (7cm) long

## Tension
26 sts x 34 rows measure 4in (10cm) square over st-st
using 3.25mm needles and DK yarn before stuffing,
or needles to give correct tension.

## Abbreviations
See page 164

## Special abbreviation
**w1** – wrap 1 stitch: take yarn between needles to opposite
side, slip one stitch pwise from LH needle to RH needle
and take yarn back between the needles to first side.

# How to make Guinea Pig

## Head and body

Using the long tail method and yarn A, cast on 12 sts.

**Row 1 and foll 2 alt rows:** Purl.
**Row 2:** *K1, m1, k4, m1, k1; rep from * once (16 sts).
**Row 4:** *K1, m1, k6, m1, k1; rep from * once (20 sts).
**Row 6:** *K1, m1, k8, m1, k1; rep from * once (24 sts).

Join on two separate balls of yarn B and rejoin yarn A and work in intarsia, twisting yarn when changing colours to avoid a hole:

**Row 7:** Yarn B-p9, yarn A-p6, and yarn B (second ball)-p9.
**Row 8:** Yarn B-(k1, m1) twice, k6, m1, k1, yarn A-k6, yarn B-k1, m1, k6, (m1, k1) twice (30 sts).
**Row 9:** Yarn B-p12, yarn A-p6, yarn B-p12.
**Row 10:** Yarn B-(k1, m1) twice, k9, m1, k1, yarn A-k6, yarn B-k1, m1, k9, (m1, k1) twice (36 sts).
**Row 11:** Yarn B-p15, yarn A-p6, yarn B-p15.
**Row 12:** Yarn B-(k1, m1) twice, k12, m1, k1, yarn A-k6, yarn B-k1, m1, k12, (m1, k1) twice (42 sts).
**Row 13:** Yarn B-p18, yarn A-p6, yarn B-p18.
**Row 14:** Yarn B-(k1, m1) twice, k14, (m1, k1) twice, yarn A-k2tog tbl, k2, k2tog, yarn B-(k1, m1) twice, k14, (m1, k1) twice (48 sts).
**Row 15:** Yarn B-p22, yarn A-p4, yarn B-p22.
**Row 16:** Yarn B-(k1, m1) twice, k19, m1, k1, yarn A-k4, yarn B-k1, m1, k19, (m1, k1) twice (54 sts).
**Row 17:** Yarn B-p25, yarn A-p4, yarn B-p25.
**Row 18:** Yarn B-(k1, m1) twice, k22, m1,

k1, yarn A-k4, yarn B-k1, m1, k22, (m1, k1) twice (60 sts).
**Row 19:** Yarn B-p28, yarn A-p4, yarn B-p28.
**Row 20:** Yarn B-k1, m1, k26, m1, k1, yarn A-k4, yarn B-k1, m1, k26, m1, k1 (64 sts).
**Row 21:** Yarn B-p30, yarn A-p4, yarn B-p30.
**Row 22:** Yarn B-k30, yarn A-k2tog tbl, k2tog, yarn B-k30 (62 sts).
**Row 23:** Cont with 1 ball of yarn B and p 1 row.
**Row 24:** K46, w1 (see special abbreviation), turn.
**Row 25:** S1p, p30, w1, turn.
**Row 26:** S1k, k to end.
**Rows 27:** Purl.
**Rows 28 to 31:** Rep rows 24 to 27 once.
**Row 32:** K16, (k2tog, k2) 8 times, k14 (54 sts).
**Rows 33 to 43:** Change to yarn A and work 11 rows in st-st.
**Rows 44 to 47:** Change to yarn B and work 4 rows in st-st.
**Row 48:** K12, (m1, k6) 6 times, k6 (60 sts).
**Rows 49 to 67:** Work 19 rows in st-st.
**Row 68:** K20, (k2tog, k4) 4 times, k16 (56 sts).
**Rows 69 to 71:** Work 3 rows in st-st.
**Row 72:** K12, (k2tog, k4) 6 times, k8 (50 sts).
**Rows 73 to 75:** Work 3 rows in st-st.
**Row 76:** K9, (k2tog, k4) 6 times, k5 (44 sts).
**Row 77 and foll alt row:** Purl.
**Row 78:** (K2tog) twice, k14, (k2tog) 4 times, k14, (k2tog) twice (36 sts).
**Row 80:** (K2tog) twice, k10, (k2tog) 4 times, k10, (k2tog) twice (28 sts).
Cast off pwise.

## Forearms and toes (make 2)

Using the long tail method and yarn B, cast on 15 sts.

**Row 1 and foll alt row:** Purl.
**Row 2:** (K2tog, k1) to end (10 sts).
**Row 4:** (K2tog) to end (5 sts).
Break yarn and thread through sts on needle, pull tight and secure by threading yarn a second time through sts.

### Toes

Using the long tail method and yarn C, cast on 12 sts.
**Rows 1 and 2:** P 1 row then k 1 row.
**Row 3:** (P2tog) to end (6 sts).
Break yarn and thread through sts on needle, pull tight and secure by threading yarn a second time through sts.

### Hind legs and toes (make 2)

Using the long tail method and yarn B, cast on 9 sts.
**Row 1:** Purl.
**Row 2:** K1, (m1, k1) to end (17 sts).
**Rows 3 to 7:** Work 5 rows in st-st.
**Row 8:** K2tog, (k1, k2tog) to end (11 sts).
**Rows 9 to 13:** Work 5 rows in st-st.
**Row 14:** K2tog, (k1, k2tog) to end (7 sts).
**Row 15:** Purl.
Break yarn and thread through sts on needle, pull tight and secure by threading yarn a second time through sts.

### Toes

Using the long tail method and yarn C, cast on 14 sts.
**Rows 1 to 3:** Beg with a p row, work 3 rows in st-st.
**Row 4:** (K2tog) to end (7 sts).
**Row 5:** Purl.
Cast off.

### Ears (make 2)

Using the long tail method and yarn D, cast on 10 sts and work in g-st.
**Rows 1 to 6:** Work 6 rows in g-st.
**Row 7:** K2tog, k6, k2tog (8 sts).
**Row 8:** Knit.
**Row 9:** K2tog, k4, k2tog (6 sts).
Cast off in g-st.

## Making up Guinea Pig

**Note:** Sew up all row-end seams on right side using mattress stitch one stitch in from the edge, unless otherwise stated; a one-stitch seam allowance has been allowed for this.

### Head and body

Run in ends around intarsia. Fold cast-off stitches in half and oversew. Sew up side edges leaving a gap, stuff and sew up gap.

### Forearms and toes

Sew up side edges of front legs, place a ball of stuffing inside and sew front legs to sides of body. Sew up side edges of toes and sew toes to forearms with toes pointing forwards.

### Hind legs and toes

Sew up side edges of hind legs, stuff and gather round cast-on stitches, pull tight and secure. Sew hind legs to sides of body. Fold cast-off stitches of toes in half and oversew. Sew up side edges of toes and sew toes to hind legs with toes pointing forwards.

### Ears

Sew cast-on stitches of ears to each side of head.

### Features

Using picture as a guide, mark position of eyes with two pins and embroider eyes in black making a vertical chain stitch for each eye, then two chain stitches on top of first. Embroider nose in dusky pink using straight stitches (see page 163 for how to begin and fasten off invisibly for the embroidery).

# How to make Guinea Pig Pups

## Head and body

**Three-colour Pups:**

**Note:** Make one pup in colours as set and one pup in colours in brackets. Using the long tail method and yarn A, (yarn B) cast on 7 sts.

**Row 1 and foll 5 alt rows:** Purl.
**Row 2:** K1, m1, k2, m1, k1, m1, k2, m1, k1 (11 sts).
**Row 4:** K1, m1, k4, m1, k1, m1, k4, m1, k1 (15 sts).
**Row 6:** K1, m1, k5, m1, k3, m1, k5, m1, k1 (19 sts).
**Row 8:** K1, m1, k7, m1, k3, m1, k7, m1, k1 (23 sts).
**Row 10:** K1, m1, k to last st, m1, k1 (25 sts).
**Row 12:** As row 10 (27 sts).
**Row 13:** Purl.
**Rows 14 and 15:** Change to yarn E (yarn A) and work 2 rows in st-st.
**Row 16:** K6, (m1, k3) 6 times, k3 (33 sts).
**Rows 17 to 19:** Work 3 rows in st-st.
**Rows 20 to 23:** Change to yarn B (yarn E) and work 4 rows in st-st.
**Row 24:** K1, (k2tog, k2) to end (25 sts).
**Row 25 and foll alt row:** Purl.
**Row 26:** K1, (k2tog, k1) to end (17 sts).
**Row 28:** K1, (k2tog) to end (9 sts).
Break yarn and thread through sts on needle, pull tight and secure by threading yarn a second time through sts.

**Two-colour Pups:**

**Note:** Make one pup in colours as set and one pup in colours in brackets. Using the long tail method and yarn B (yarn E), cast on 7 sts.

**Row 1 and foll 4 alt rows:** Purl.
**Row 2:** K1, m1, k2, m1, k1, m1, k2, m1, k1 (11 sts).
**Row 4:** K1, m1, k4, m1, k1, m1, k4, m1, k1 (15 sts).
**Row 6:** K1, m1, k5, m1, k3, m1, k5, m1, k1 (19 sts).
**Row 8:** K1, m1, k7, m1, k3, m1, k7, m1, k1 (23 sts).
**Row 10:** K1, m1, k to last st, m1, k1 (25 sts).
**Row 11:** Purl.
**Row 12:** K1, m1, k to last st, m1, k1 (27 sts).
**Rows 13 to 15:** Change to yarn A (yarn B) and work 3 rows in st-st.
**Row 16:** K6, (m1, k3) 6 times, k3 (33 sts).
**Rows 17 to 23:** Work 7 rows in st-st.
**Row 24:** K1, (k2tog, k2) to end (25 sts).
**Row 25 and foll alt row:** Purl.
**Row 26:** K1, (k2tog, k1) to end (17 sts).
**Row 28:** K1, (k2tog) to end (9 sts).
Break yarn and thread through sts on needle, pull tight and secure by threading yarn a second time through sts.

## Forearms and hind legs
(make 2 forearms in colour to match head of Pup and 2 hind legs in colour to match rear of each Pup)

Using the long tail method and yarn required, cast on 8 sts.

**Rows 1 to 3:** Work 3 rows in st-st.
Break yarn and thread through sts, pull tight and secure by threading yarn a second time through sts.

## Ears (make 2 for each pup)

Using the long tail method and yarn D, cast on 5 sts and work in g-st.
**Rows 1 and 2:** Work 2 rows in g-st.
**Row 3:** K2tog, k1, k2tog (3 sts).
Cast off in g-st.

# Making up Guinea Pig Pups

**Note:** Sew up all row-end seams on right side using mattress stitch one stitch in from the edge, unless otherwise stated; a one-stitch seam allowance has been allowed for this.

## Head and body
Sew up side edges of head and body leaving a gap, stuff and close gap.

## Forearms and hind legs
Sew up side edges of forearms and sew cast-on stitches to front of body. Sew up side edges of hind legs, gather round cast-on stitches, pull tight and secure. Sew hind legs parallel to body.

## Ears
Sew cast-on stitches of ears to each side of head.

## Features
Using picture as a guide, mark position of eyes with two pins and embroider eyes in black making a vertical chain stitch for each eye, then a second chain stitch on top of first (see page 163 for how to begin and fasten off invisibly for the embroidery).

# Beaver

# Information you'll need

## Materials
Any DK (US: light worsted) yarn
(amounts given are approximate)
**Yarn A** dark brown (60g)
**Yarn B** brown (20g)
**Yarn C** white (5g)
Oddment of black for embroidery
1 pair of 3.25mm (UK10:US3) needles
Knitters' pins and a blunt-ended needle for sewing up
Acrylic toy stuffing
Piece of stiff cardboard

## Finished size
Beaver measures 6¾in (17cm) high

## Tension
26 sts x 34 rows measure 4in (10cm) square over
st-st using 3.25mm needles and DK yarn before
stuffing, or needles to give correct tension.

## Abbreviations
See page 164

## Special abbreviation
**w1** – wrap 1 stitch: take yarn between needles to
opposite side, slip one stitch pwise from LH needle
to RH needle and take yarn back between the
needles to first side.

# How to make Beaver

## Body and head

Using the long tail method and yarn A, cast on 28 sts and place a marker at centre of cast-on edge.

**Row 1 and foll 5 alt rows:** Purl.
**Row 2:** K3, m1, (k2, m1) to last 3 sts, k3 (40 sts).
**Row 4:** K6, m1, (k4, m1) 7 times, k6 (48 sts).
**Row 6:** K10, m1, (k4, m1) 7 times, k10 (56 sts).
**Row 8:** K7, (m1, k6) 8 times, k1 (64 sts).
**Row 10:** K4, m1, (k8, m1) 7 times, k4 (72 sts).
**Row 12:** K8, (m1, k8) to end (80 sts).
**Row 13:** Purl.
**Row 14:** K65, w1 (see special abbreviation), turn.
**Row 15:** S1p, p50, w1, turn.
**Row 16:** S1k, k to end.
**Rows 17 to 19:** Work 3 rows in st-st.
**Rows 20 to 43:** Rep rows 14 to 19, 4 times more.
**Row 44:** *K7, k2tog, k2, k2tog, k7; rep from * 3 times more (72 sts).
**Rows 45 to 47:** Work 3 rows in st-st.
**Row 48:** *K6, k2tog, k2, k2tog, k6; rep from * 3 times more (64 sts).
**Rows 49 to 51:** Work 3 rows in st-st.
**Row 52:** *K5, k2tog, k2, k2tog, k5; rep from * 3 times more (56 sts).
**Rows 53 to 55:** Work 3 rows in st-st.
**Row 56:** *K2, (k2tog) twice, k2; rep from * 6 times more (42 sts).
**Row 57:** Purl.
**Row 58:** K35, w1, turn.
**Row 59:** S1p, p28, w1, turn.
**Row 60:** S1k, k to end.
**Row 61:** Purl.
**Row 62:** K16, (m1, k2) 6 times, k14 (48 sts).
**Rows 63 to 65:** Work 3 rows in st-st.

**Row 66:** K40, w1, turn.
**Row 67:** S1p, p32, w1, turn.
**Row 68:** S1k, k to end.
**Rows 69 to 71:** Work 3 rows in st-st.
**Rows 72 to 77:** Rep rows 66 to 71 once.
**Row 78:** K20, (k2tog) 4 times, k20 (44 sts).
**Row 79 and 4 foll alt rows:** Purl.
**Row 80:** K18, (k2tog) 4 times, k18 (40 sts).
**Row 82:** K16, (k2tog) 4 times, k16 (36 sts).
**Row 84:** K14, (k2tog) 4 times, k14 (32 sts).
**Row 86:** (K2tog) twice, k8, (k2tog) 4 times, k8, (k2tog) twice (24 sts).
**Row 88:** (K2tog) twice, k4, (k2tog) 4 times, k4, (k2tog) twice (16 sts).
**Row 89:** Purl.
Cast off.

## Tail (make 2 pieces)

Using the long tail method and yarn B, cast on 10 sts and work in g-st.
**Row 1:** Knit.
**Row 2:** K1, m1, k to last st, m1, k1 (12 sts).
**Rows 3 to 7:** Work 5 rows in g-st.
**Rows 8 to 26:** Rep rows 2 to 7, 3 times more then row 2 once (20 sts).
**Rows 27 to 40:** Work 14 rows in g-st.
**Row 41:** K2tog, k to last 2 sts, k2tog (18 sts).
**Row 42:** Knit.

**Rows 43 to 46:** Rep rows 41 and 42 twice more (14 sts).
**Row 47:** (K2tog) twice, k6, (k2tog) twice (10 sts).
**Row 48:** Knit.
**Rows 49:** (K2tog) twice, k2, (k2tog) twice (6 sts).
Cast off in g-st.

## Hind legs (make 2)

Using the long tail method and yarn A, cast on 14 sts.
**Row 1:** Purl.
**Row 2:** K2, (m1, k2) to end (20 sts).
**Rows 3 to 15:** Work 13 rows in st-st.
**Row 16:** K4, (k2tog) 6 times, k4, (14 sts).
**Rows 17 to 21:** Work 5 rows in st-st.
**Row 22:** (K2tog) to end (7 sts).
Break yarn and thread through sts on needle, pull tight and secure by threading yarn a second time through sts.

## Forearms (make 2)

Using the long tail method and yarn A, cast on 12 sts.

**Row 1:** Purl.

**Row 2:** K3, (m1, k2) to last 3 sts, m1, k3 (16 sts).

**Rows 3 to 7:** Work 5 rows in st-st.

**Row 8:** K2tog, k to last 2 sts, k2tog (14 sts).

**Row 9:** Purl.

**Rows 10 to 13:** Rep rows 8 and 9 twice more (10 sts).

**Row 14:** (K2tog) twice, k2, (k2tog) twice (6 sts).

Cast off pwise.

## Ears (make 2)

Using the long tail method and yarn A, cast on 7 sts.

**Row 1:** Purl.

**Row 2:** K1, (m1, k1) to end (13 sts).

**Rows 3 to 7:** Work 5 rows in st-st.

**Row 8:** K1, (k2tog, k1) to end (9 sts).

Break yarn and thread through sts on needle, pull tight and secure by threading yarn a second time through sts.

## Teeth

Using the long tail method and yarn C, cast on 8 sts.

**Rows 1 to 5:** Beg with a p row, work 5 rows in st-st.

Cast off.

## Making up Beaver

**Note:** Sew up all row-end seams on right side using mattress stitch one stitch in from the edge, unless otherwise stated; a one-stitch seam allowance has been allowed for this.

### Head and body

Fold cast-off stitches in half and oversew. Sew up side edges leaving a gap. Bring seam and marker together and oversew cast-on stitches. Stuff and sew up gap.

### Tail

Place tail on thick cardboard and draw round outside edge. Draw a line ¼in (6mm) inside line and cut out. Sandwich cardboard between two pieces of tail and oversew around outside edge, enclosing cardboard inside. Sew tail to back of beaver.

### Hind legs

Sew up side edges of hind legs, stuff, then sew across cast-on stitches. Assemble Beaver on a flat surface and sew hind legs to Beaver.

### Forearms

Sew up straight edges of forearms, stuff, and pin and sew forearms to Beaver.

### Ears

Sew up side edges of ears and with this seam at centre back, sew ears to Beaver.

### Teeth and features

Oversew side edges of teeth and with this seam at centre of inside edge, sew top of teeth to Beaver and sew between middle of teeth. Using picture as a guide, mark position of eyes with two pins and embroider eyes in black making a vertical chain stitch for each eye, then a second chain stitch on top of first (see page 163 for how to begin and fasten off invisibly for the embroidery).

# Seahorse

# Information you'll need

## Materials

Any DK (US: light worsted) yarn
(amounts given are approximate)
**Yarn A** turquoise (40g)
**Yarn B** plum (20g)
Oddment of black for embroidery
1 pair of 3.25mm (UK10:US3) needles and a spare
needle of the same size
Knitters' pins and a blunt-ended needle for sewing up
Tweezers (optional)
1 chenille stem (approx. 12in/30cm long)
Acrylic toy stuffing

## Finished size

Seahorse measures 11in (28cm) high

## Tension

26 sts x 34 rows measure 4in (10cm) square over st-st
using 3.25mm needles and DK yarn before stuffing,
or needles to give correct tension.

## Abbreviations

See page 164

## Special abbreviation

**w1** – wrap 1 stitch: take yarn between needles to
opposite side, slip one stitch pwise from LH needle
to RH needle and take yarn back between the
needles to first side.

# How to make Seahorse

## Tail, body and head

Using the long tail method and yarn A, cast on 5 sts.
**Row 1:** Purl.
Join on yarn B and work in yarn A and B, carrying yarn loosely up side of work, as foll:
**Rows 2 and 3:** Yarn B-work 2 rows in g-st.
**Rows 4 and 5:** Yarn A-k 1 row then p 1 row.
**Row 6:** Yarn B-k1, m1, k to last st, m1, k1 (7 sts).
**Row 7:** Yarn B-knit.
**Rows 8 and 9:** Yarn A-k 1 row then p 1 row.
**Rows 10 and 11:** Yarn B-work 2 rows in g-st.
**Rows 12 to 17:** Rep rows 8 to 11 once, then rows 8 and 9 once.
**Rows 18 to 65:** Rep rows 6 to 17, 4 times more (15 sts).
**Row 66:** Yarn A-k1, m1, k to last st, m1, k1 (17 sts).
**Row 67:** Yarn A-purl.
**Row 68:** Yarn B-(k1, m1) twice, k to last 2 sts, (m1, k1) twice (21 sts).
**Row 69:** Yarn B-knit.
**Rows 70 and 71:** Yarn A-k 1 row then p 1 row.
**Row 72:** Yarn A-(k1, m1) twice, k to last 2 sts, (m1, k1) twice (25 sts).
**Row 73:** Yarn A-purl.
**Rows 74 and 75:** Yarn B-rep rows 68 and 69 once (29 sts).
**Row 76:** Yarn A-(k4, s1p) twice, k9, (s1p, k4) twice.
**Row 77:** Yarn A-(p4, s1p) twice, p9, (s1p, p4) twice.
**Row 78:** Yarn A-(k1, m1) twice, k2, s1p, k4, s1p, k9, s1p, k4, s1p, k2, (m1, k1) twice (33 sts).
**Row 79:** Yarn A-p6, s1p, p4, s1p, p9, s1p, p4, s1p, p6.
**Row 80:** Yarn B-k1, m1, k4, m1, k23, m1, k4, m1, k1 (37 sts).

**Row 81:** Yarn B-knit.
**Row 82:** Yarn A-k3, s1p, (k4, s1p) twice, k9, (s1p, k4) twice, s1p, k3.
**Row 83:** Yarn A-p3, s1p, (p4, s1p) twice, p9, (s1p, p4) twice, s1p, p3.
**Row 84:** Yarn A-k1, m1, k2, s1p, k3, m1, k1, s1p, k4, s1p, k9, s1p, k4, s1p, k1, m1, k3, s1p, k2, m1, k1 (41 sts).
**Row 85:** Yarn A-p4, s1p, p5, s1p, p4, s1p, p9, s1p, p4, s1p, p5, s1p, p4.
**Row 86:** Yarn B-k9, m1, k23, m1, k9 (43 sts).
**Row 87:** Yarn B-knit.
**Row 88:** Yarn A-k4, s1p, k6, s1p, k4, s1p, k9, s1p, k4, s1p, k6, s1p, k4.
**Row 89:** Yarn A-p4, s1p, p6, s1p, p4, s1p, p9, s1p, p4, s1p, p6, s1p, p4.
**Row 90:** Yarn A-k1, m1, k3, s1p, k6, s1p, k4, s1p, k9, s1p, k4, s1p, k6, s1p, k3, m1, k1 (45 sts).
**Row 91:** Yarn A-p5, s1p, p6, s1p, p4, s1p, p9, s1p, p4, s1p, p6, s1p, p5.
**Rows 92 and 93:** Yarn B-work 2 rows in g-st.
**Row 94:** Yarn A-k5, s1p, k6, s1p, k4, s1p, k9, s1p, k4, s1p, k6, s1p, k5.
**Row 95:** Yarn A-p5, s1p, p6, s1p, p4, s1p, p9, s1p, p4, s1p, p6, s1p, p5.
**Rows 96 and 97:** Rep rows 94 and 95 once.
**Rows 98 and 99:** Yarn B-work 2 rows in g-st.
**Rows 100 to 107:** Rep rows 94 to 99 once, then rows 94 and 95 once.
**Row 108:** Yarn A-k2tog, k3, s1p, k2tog, (k4, s1p) twice, k9, (s1p, k4) twice, k2tog, s1p, k3, k2tog (41 sts).
**Row 109:** Yarn A-p4, s1p, p5, s1p, p4, s1p, p9, s1p, p4, s1p, p5, s1p, p4.

**Row 110:** Yarn B-k2tog, k4, k2tog, k25, k2tog, k4, k2tog (37 sts).
**Row 111:** Yarn B-knit.
**Row 112:** Yarn A-k8, s1p, k4, s1p, k9, s1p, k4, s1p, k8.
**Row 113:** Yarn A-p8, s1p, p4, s1p, p9, s1p, p4, s1p, p8.
**Row 114:** Yarn A-(k2tog) twice, (k4, s1p) twice, k9, (s1p, k4) twice, (k2tog) twice (33 sts).
**Row 115:** Yarn A-p6, s1p, p4, s1p, p9, s1p, p4, s1p, p6.
**Row 116:** Yarn B-(k2tog) twice, k to last 4 sts, (k2tog) twice (29 sts).
**Row 117:** Yarn B-knit.
**Row 118:** Yarn A-k2tog, k to last 2 sts, k2tog (27 sts).
**Row 119:** Yarn A-Purl.
**Rows 120 and 121:** Rep rows 118 and 119 once (25 sts).
**Rows 122 and 123:** Rep rows 116 and 117 once (21 sts).
**Row 124:** Yarn A-k2tog, k to last 2 sts, k2tog (19 sts).
**Row 125:** Yarn A-p15, w1 (see special abbreviation), turn.
**Row 126:** Yarn A-s1p, k11, w1, turn.
**Row 127:** Yarn A-s1p, p to end.
**Rows 128 and 129:** Yarn B-work 2 rows in g-st.
**Row 130:** Yarn A-knit.
**Row 131:** Yarn A-p14, w1, turn.
**Row 132:** Yarn A-s1p, k9, w1, turn.
**Row 133:** Yarn A-s1p, p to end.
**Rows 134 and 135:** Yarn B-work 2 rows in g-st.
**Row 136:** Yarn A-knit.
**Row 137:** Yarn A-p13, w1, turn.
**Row 138:** Yarn A-s1p, k7, w1, turn.
**Row 139:** Yarn A-s1p, p to end.
**Rows 140 and 141:** Yarn B-work 2 rows in g-st.
**Row 142:** Yarn A-knit.
**Row 143:** Yarn A-p15, w1, turn.

**Row 144:** Yarn A-s1p, k11, w1, turn.
**Row 145:** Yarn A-s1p, p to end.
**Rows 146 and 147:** Yarn B-work 2 rows in g-st.
**Row 148:** Yarn A-k1, m1, k to last st, m1, k1 (21 sts).
**Row 149:** Yarn A-p17, w1, turn.
**Row 150:** Yarn A-s1p, k13, w1, k1.
**Row 151:** Yarn A-s1p, p to end.
**Row 152:** Yarn A-k1, m1, k to last st, m1, k1 (23 sts).
**Row 153:** Yarn A-p19, w1, turn.
**Row 154:** Yarn A-s1p, k15, w1, turn.
**Row 155:** Yarn A-s1p, p to end.
**Row 156:** Yarn B-k1, m1, k to last st, m1, k1 (25 sts).
**Row 157:** Yarn B-knit.
**Row 158:** Yarn A-k1, m1, k to last st, m1, k1 (27 sts).
**Row 159:** Yarn A-p9, (p2tog) twice, p1, (p2tog) twice, p9 (23 sts).
**Row 160:** Yarn A-k1, m1, k8, k2tog, k1, k2tog, k8, m1, k1.
**Row 161:** Yarn A-p7, (p2tog) twice, p1, (p2tog) twice p7 (19 sts).
**Row 162:** Yarn A-k1, m1, k6, k2tog, k1, k2tog, k6, m1, k1.
**Row 163:** Yarn A-p5, (p2tog) twice, p1, (p2tog) twice p5 (15 sts).
**Row 164:** Yarn A-k1, m1, k4, k2tog, k1, k2tog, k4, m1, k1.
**Row 165:** Yarn A-purl.
**Rows 166 to 168:** Rep rows 164 and 165 once, then row 164 once.
**Row 169:** Yarn B (Rejoin yarn B)-purl. Cont in yarn B and shape:
**Row 170:** K8, w1, turn.
**Row 171:** S1p, p1, w1, turn.
**Row 172:** S1p, k2, w1, turn.
**Row 173:** S1p, p3, w1, turn.
**Row 174:** S1p, k4, w1, turn.
**Row 175:** S1p, p5, w1, turn.
**Row 176:** S1p, k6, w1, turn.
**Row 177:** S1p, p7, w1, turn.

**Row 178:** S1p, k8, w1, turn.
**Row 179:** S1p, p9, w1, turn.
**Row 180:** S1p, k10, w1, turn.
**Row 181:** S1p, p11, w1, turn.
**Row 182:** S1p, k2tog, (k1, k2tog) 3 times, k2 (11 sts).
**Row 183:** P2tog, (p1, p2tog) to end (7 sts). Break yarn and thread yarn through sts on needle, pull tight and secure by threading yarn a second time through sts.

## Fins (make 2)
Using the long tail method and yarn B, cast on 18 sts.
**Row 1:** Purl.
Join on yarn A and work in yarn A and B carrying yarn loosely up side of work, as foll:
**Row 2:** Yarn A-p6, s1p, p4, s1p, p6.
**Row 3:** Yarn A-k6, s1p, k4, s1p, k6.
**Rows 4 and 5:** Rep rows 2 and 3 once.
**Rows 6 and 7:** Yarn B-p 2 rows.
**Row 8:** Yarn A-p6, s1p, p4, s1p, p6.
**Row 9:** Yarn A-k3, m1, k3, s1p, k4, s1p, k3, m1, k3 (20 sts).
**Row 10:** Yarn A-p7, s1p, p4, s1p, p7.
**Row 11:** Yarn A-k3, m1, k1, m1, k3, s1p, k1, m1, k2, m1, k1, s1p, k3, m1, k1, m1, k3 (26 sts).
**Rows 12 and 13:** Yarn B-p 2 rows.
**Row 14:** Yarn A-purl.
**Row 15:** Yarn A-k4, m1, k1, m1, k16, m1, k1, m1, k4 (30 sts).
**Row 16:** Yarn A-purl.
**Row 17:** Yarn A-k1, (m1, k4) to last st, m1, k1 (38 sts).
**Rows 18 and 19:** Cont in yarn B and p 2 rows. Cast off kwise.

## Making up Seahorse

**Note:** Sew up all row-end seams on right side using mattress stitch one stitch in from the edge, unless otherwise stated; a one-stitch seam allowance has been allowed for this.

### Tail, body and head
Gather round cast-on stitches of tail, fold chenille stem in half and place fold into wrong side of gathered stitches. Sew up row ends of tail along its length enclosing chenille stem inside. Stuff base of tail with tweezers or tip of scissors. Sew up row ends of nose, head and neck and stuff. Sew up row ends of body leaving a gap, stuff and sew up gap. Curl tip of tail around.

### Fins
Sew up row ends of fins and with this seam at centre of inside edge, oversew cast-on then cast-off stitches. Sew fins to Seahorse.

### Features
Using picture as a guide, mark position of eyes with two pins and embroider eyes in black making a vertical chain stitch for each eye, then a second chain stitch on top of first (see page 163 for how to begin and fasten off invisibly for the embroidery).

# Walrus

# Information you'll need

## Materials
Any DK (US: light worsted) yarn
(amounts given are approximate)
**Yarn A** ginger (60g)
**Yarn B** dark grey (5g)
**Yarn C** cream (5g)
Oddment of black for embroidery
1 pair of 3.25mm (UK10:US3) needles
Knitters' pins and a blunt-ended needle for sewing up
Acrylic toy stuffing
2 white chenille stems

## Finished size
Walrus measures 11in (28cm) long

## Tension
26 sts x 34 rows measure 4in (10cm) square over st-st
using 3.25mm needles and DK yarn before stuffing,
or needles to give correct tension.

## Abbreviations
See page 164

# How to make Walrus

## Body and head

Using the long tail method and yarn A, cast on 82 sts.

**Row 1 and foll alt row:** Purl.
**Row 2:** K36, (m1, k2) 6 times, k34 (88 sts).
**Row 4:** K39, (m1, k2) 6 times, k37 (94 sts).
**Rows 5 to 7:** Work 3 rows in st-st.
**Row 8:** K42, (m1, k2) 6 times, k40 (100 sts).
**Rows 9 to 27:** Work 19 rows in st-st.
**Rows 28 to 39:** Cast off 4 sts at beg of next 12 rows (52 sts).
**Row 40:** K2tog, k to last 2 sts, k2tog (50 sts).
**Row 41:** Purl.
**Rows 42:** As row 40 (48 sts).
**Rows 43 to 59:** Work 17 rows in st-st.
**Row 60:** (K2tog, k4) to end (40 sts).
**Row 61 and foll 3 alt rows:** Purl.
**Row 62:** (K2tog, k3) to end (32 sts).
**Row 64:** (K2tog, k2) to end (24 sts).
**Row 66:** (K2tog, k1) to end (16 sts).
**Row 68:** (K2tog) to end (8 sts).
Break yarn and thread through sts on needle, pull tight and secure by threading yarn a second time through sts.

## Tail (make 2 pieces)

Using the long tail method and yarn A, cast on 20 sts.

**Row 1:** Purl.
**Row 2:** (K1, m1, k8, m1, k1) twice (24 sts).
**Rows 3 to 17:** Beg with a p row, work 15 rows in st-st.
**Row 18:** K2tog, k to last 2 sts, k2tog (22 sts).
**Row 19:** P2tog, p to last 2 sts, p2tog (20 sts).
**Rows 20 to 27:** Rep rows 18 and 19, 4 times more (4 sts).
Cast off.

## Front flippers (make 2)

Using the long tail method and yarn A, cast on 40 sts.

**Rows 1 to 3:** Beg with a p row, work 3 rows in st-st.
**Row 4:** K4, (k2tog, k4) to end (34 sts).
**Row 5:** Purl.
**Row 6:** K2tog, k to last 2 sts, k2tog (32 sts).
**Row 7:** P2tog, p to last 2 sts, p2tog (30 sts).
**Rows 8 to 13:** Rep rows 6 and 7, 3 times more (18 sts).
Place a marker on first and last st of last row.

**Rows 14 and 15:** Work 2 rows in st-st.
**Row 16:** K2tog, k to last 2 sts, k2tog (16 sts).
**Row 17:** P2tog, p to last 2 sts, p2tog (14 sts).
**Rows 18 to 21:** Rep rows 16 and 17 twice more (6 sts).
Cast off.

## Snout

Using the long tail method and yarn B, cast on 32 sts.

**Row 1 and foll 4 alt rows:** Purl.
**Row 2:** K2tog, k6, k2tog, k12, k2tog, k6, k2tog (28 sts).
**Row 4:** K2tog, k5, k2tog, k10, k2tog, k5, k2tog (24 sts).
**Row 6:** K2tog, k4, k2tog, k8, k2tog, k4, k2tog (20 sts).
**Row 8:** K2tog, k3, k2tog, k6, k2tog, k3, k2tog (16 sts).
**Row 10:** (K2tog) to end (8 sts).
Break yarn and thread through sts on needle, pull tight and secure by threading yarn a second time through sts.

### Teeth (make 2)

Using the long tail method and yarn C, cast on 7 sts.

**Rows 1 to 25:** Beg with a p row, work 25 rows in st-st.

Break yarn and thread through sts on needle, pull tight and secure by threading yarn a second time through sts.

## Making up Walrus

**Note:** Sew up all row-end seams on right side using mattress stitch one stitch in from the edge, unless otherwise stated; a one-stitch seam allowance has been allowed for this.

### Body and head

Sew up row ends of head and along back. Fold cast-on stitches in half and oversew leaving a gap, stuff head. Bring two seams together at tail and oversew across stitches. Stuff body and sew up gap.

### Tail

Fold cast-on stitches of two pieces of tail in half and oversew. Sew up side edges from lower edge to decrease stitches. Stuff two pieces of tail and sew to Walrus.

### Front flippers

Fold cast-on stitches of flippers in half and oversew. Sew up side edges as far as markers. Stuff flippers and pin and sew to Walrus.

### Snout

Sew up side edges of snout, stuff then pin and sew to face.

### Teeth

Fold chenille stems in half and place fold into stitches pulled tight on a thread. Sew up side edges of teeth enclosing chenille stems inside. Cut chenille stems to length of teeth and sew teeth to Walrus.

### Features

Using picture as a guide, mark position of eyes with two pins and embroider eyes in black making a vertical chain stitch for each eye, then a second chain stitch on top of first (see page 163 for how to begin and fasten off invisibly for the embroidery).

# Lobster

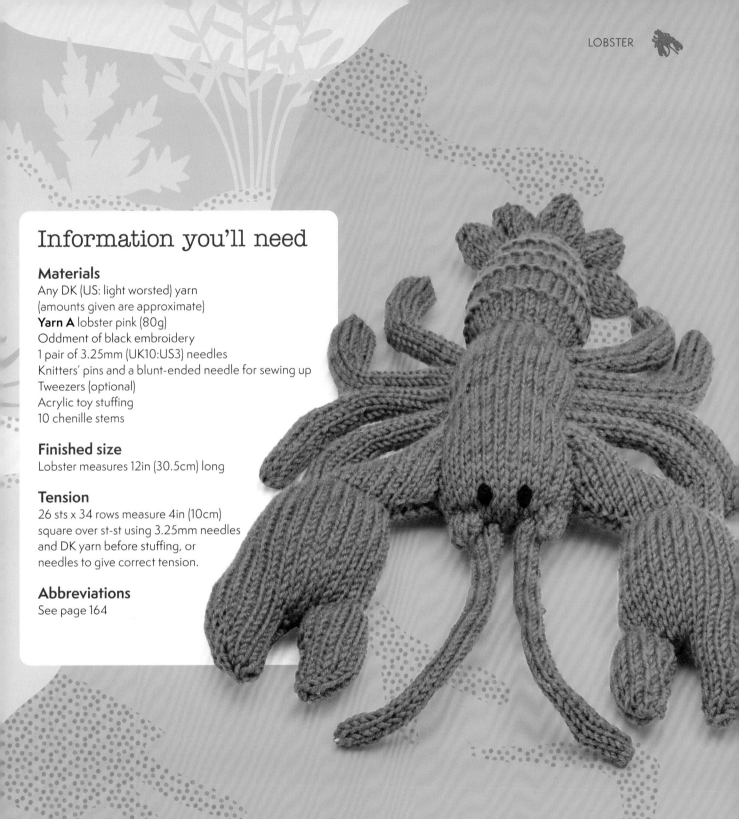

# Information you'll need

## Materials
Any DK (US: light worsted) yarn
(amounts given are approximate)
**Yarn A** lobster pink (80g)
Oddment of black embroidery
1 pair of 3.25mm (UK10:US3) needles
Knitters' pins and a blunt-ended needle for sewing up
Tweezers (optional)
Acrylic toy stuffing
10 chenille stems

## Finished size
Lobster measures 12in (30.5cm) long

## Tension
26 sts x 34 rows measure 4in (10cm)
square over st-st using 3.25mm needles
and DK yarn before stuffing, or
needles to give correct tension.

## Abbreviations
See page 164

## How to make Lobster

### Body and head
Using the long tail method and yarn A, cast on 24 sts.
**Row 1:** Purl.
**Row 2:** K3, (m1, k2) 4 times, k2, (k2, m1) 4 times, k3 (32 sts).
**Rows 3 to 17:** Beg with a p row, work 15 rows in st-st.
**Row 18:** *K4, (k2tog) 4 times, k4; rep from * once (24 sts).
**Row 19:** Purl.
**Row 20:** K4, (m1, k1) twice, (k1, m1) twice, k8, (m1, k1) twice, (k1, m1) twice, k4 (32 sts).
**Rows 21 to 27:** Work 7 rows in st-st.
**Row 28:** *K6, (k2tog) twice, k6; rep from * once (28 sts).
**Row 29 and foll alt row:** Purl.
**Row 30:** *K5, (k2tog) twice, k5; rep from * once (24 sts).
**Row 32:** *K4, (k2tog) twice, k4; rep from * once (20 sts).
**Row 33:** Purl.
Cast off.

### Rear body
Using the long tail method and yarn A, cast on 28 sts.
**Rows 1 to 4:** Beg with a k row, work 4 rows in st-st.
**Rows 5 and 6:** P 2 rows.
**Rows 7 and 8:** K 1 row then p 1 row.
**Rows 9 and 10:** Work 2 rows in g-st.
**Rows 11 to 16:** Rep rows 1 to 6 once.
**Row 17:** K4, (k2tog) twice, k12, (k2tog) twice, k4 (24 sts).
**Row 18:** Purl.
**Rows 19 and 20:** Work 2 rows in g-st.
**Rows 21 and 22:** K 1 row then p 1 row.
**Row 23:** K3, (k2tog) twice, k10, (k2tog) twice, k3 (20 sts).
**Rows 24 to 26:** P 3 rows.
**Row 27:** K2, (k2tog) twice, k8, (k2tog) twice, k2 (16 sts).
**Row 28:** Purl.
**Rows 29 and 30:** Work 2 rows in g-st. Cast off kwise.

### Front legs (make 2)
Using the long tail method and yarn A, cast on 16 sts.
**Rows 1 to 3:** Beg with a p row work 3 rows in st-st.
**Row 4:** K1, m1, k5, (k2tog) twice, k5, m1, k1.
**Row 5:** Purl.
**Rows 6 to 11:** Rep rows 4 and 5, 3 times more.
**Row 12:** K2tog, k to last 2 sts, k2tog (14 sts).
**Row 13:** Purl.
**Row 14 to 21:** Rep rows 12 and 13, 4 times more (6 sts).
Cast off.

### Pincers (make 2)
#### Large piece
Using the long tail method and yarn A, cast on 12 sts.
**Row 1 and foll alt row:** Purl.
**Row 2:** *(K1, m1) twice, k2, (m1, k1) twice; rep from * once (20 sts).
**Row 4:** *(K1, m1) twice, k6, (m1, k1) twice; rep from * once (28 sts).
**Rows 5 to 21:** Beg with a p row, work 17 rows in st-st.
**Row 22:** K2tog, k11, m1, k2, m1, k11, k2tog.
**Row 23:** P2tog, p to last 2 sts, p2tog (26 sts).
**Row 24:** Cast off 4 sts, k17 (18 sts now on RH needle), cast off 4 sts and fasten off (18 sts).

Rejoin yarn to rem sts and dec:
**Row 25:** P2tog, p to last 2 sts, p2tog (16 sts).
**Rows 26 to 29:** Work 4 rows in st-st.
**Row 30:** K5, k2tog, k2, k2tog, k5 (14 st).
**Row 31 and foll 2 alt rows:** Purl.
**Row 32:** K4, k2tog, k2, k2tog, k4 (12 sts).
**Row 34:** K4, (k2tog) twice, k4 (10 sts).
**Row 36:** (K2tog) to end (5 sts).
Break yarn and thread through sts on needle, pull tight and secure by threading yarn a second time through sts.

#### Small piece
Using the long tail method and yarn A, cast on 10 sts.
**Row 1:** Purl.
**Row 2:** (K1, m1, k3, m1, k1) twice (14 sts).
**Rows 3 to 7:** Beg with a p row, work 5 rows in st-st.
**Row 8:** K2tog, k to last 2 sts, k2tog (12 sts).
**Rows 9 to 11:** Beg with a p row, work 3 rows in st-st.
**Row 12:** K4, (k2tog) twice, k4 (10 sts).
**Row 13 and foll alt row:** Purl.
**Row 14:** K3, (k2tog) twice, k3 (8 sts).
**Row 16:** (K2tog) to end (4 sts).
Break yarn and thread through sts on needle, pull tight and secure by threading yarn a second time through sts.

## Tail (make 5 pieces)

Using the long tail method and yarn A, cast on 8 sts.

**Rows 1 to 3:** Beg with a p row, work 3 rows in st-st.

**Row 4:** K1, (m1, k1) to end (15 sts).

**Rows 5 to 7:** Work 3 rows in st-st.

**Row 8:** (K2tog, k1) to end (10 sts).

**Row 9:** Purl.

**Row 10:** (K2tog) to end (5 sts).

Break yarn and thread through sts on needle, pull tight and secure by threading yarn a second time through sts.

## Legs (make 8)

Using the long tail method and yarn A, cast on 9 sts.

**Rows 1 to 13:** Beg with a p row work 13 rows in st-st.

**Row 14:** K3, (m1, k3) twice (11 sts).

**Rows 15 to 19:** Work 5 rows in st-st.

**Row 20:** K4, m1, k3, m1, k4 (13 sts).

**Rows 21 to 27:** Work 7 rows in st-st.

**Row 28:** K1, (k2tog, k1) to end (9 sts).

Break yarn and thread through sts on needle, pull tight and secure by threading yarn a second time through sts.

## Antennas (make 2)

Using the long tail method and yarn A, cast on 9 sts.

**Row 1:** Purl.

**Row 2:** (K2tog, k1) to end (6 sts).

**Row 3:** Purl.

Break yarn and thread through sts on needle, pull tight and secure by threading yarn a second time through sts.

## Tentacles (make 2)

Using the long tail method and yarn A, cast on 8 sts.

Beg with a p row, work in st-st until piece measures 5in (12.5cm).

Break yarn and thread through sts on needle, pull tight and secure by threading yarn a second time through sts.

# Making up Lobster

**Note:** Sew up all row-end seams on right side using mattress stitch one stitch in from the edge, unless otherwise stated; a one-stitch seam allowance has been allowed for this.

## Body, head and rear body

Sew up row ends of body and head and with this seam at centre of underneath, sew across cast-on stitches. Stuff body and head. Sew up row ends of rear body and with this seam at centre of underneath, sew across cast-off stitches. Stuff rear body and sew cast-on stitches to body.

## Front legs and pincers

Fold cast-on stitches of front legs in half and oversew. Sew up increasing row ends and stuff. Sew open end of front legs to head at each side. Sew up row ends of pincers, stuff, pushing stuffing into tips with tweezers or tip of scissors. Fold cast-on stitches in half and oversew. Sew pincers to ends of front legs. Sew up row ends of small piece, stuff, pushing stuffing in with tweezers or tip of scissors. Fold cast-on stitches in half and oversew. Sew small pieces to pincers.

## Tail

Sew up side edges of tail pieces and with seam at centre back, flatten pieces. Sew tail pieces to Lobster fanning out the tail.

## Legs

Take a chenille stem for each leg and fold in half, then fold over tip for wide part of ends of legs. Place folded chenille stems on wrong side of legs and sew up side edges enclosing chenille stems inside. Sew legs along sides of rear body, four on each side and bend legs.

## Antennas and tentacles

Sew up row ends of antennas and sew cast-on stitches to sides of head. Place a chenille stem on wrong side of tentacles and sew up side edges. Cut chenille stem to length of tentacle, sew tentacles to Lobster and bend tips down.

## Features

Using picture as a guide, mark position of eyes with two pins and embroider eyes in black making a chain stitch for each eye, then a second chain stitch on top of first (see page 163 for how to begin and fasten off invisibly for the embroidery).

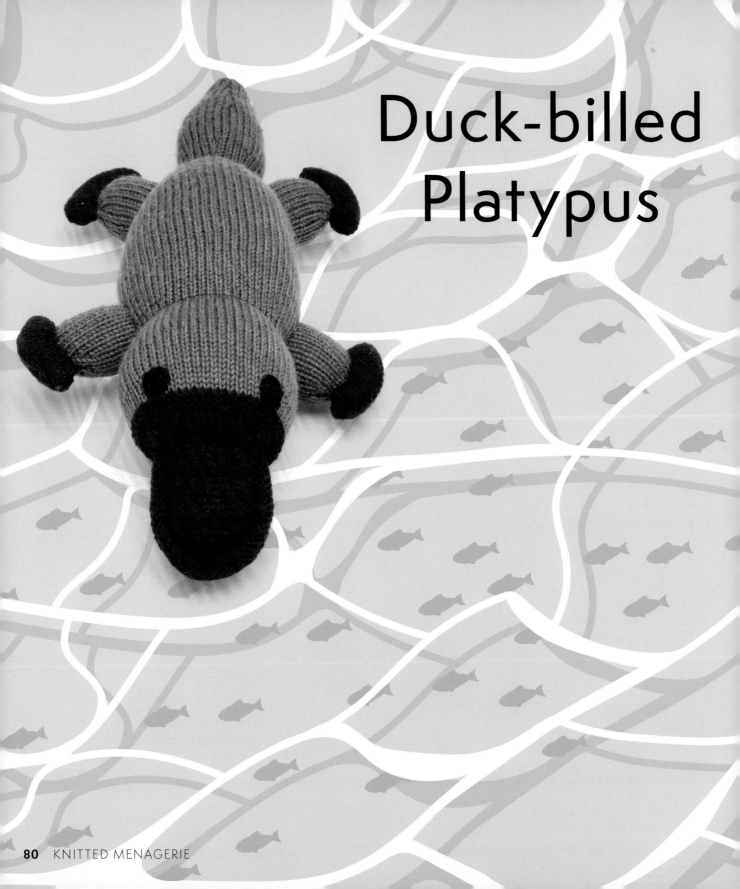

# Duck-billed Platypus

# Information you'll need

## Materials

Any DK (US: light worsted) yarn
(amounts given are approximate)
**Yarn A** brown (50g)
**Yarn B** beige (20g)
**Yarn C** dark brown (20g)
Oddment of black for embroidery
1 pair of 3.25mm (UK10:US3) needles
A blunt-ended needle for sewing up
Tweezers (optional)
Acrylic toy stuffing

## Finished size

Duck-billed Platypus measures
16in (41cm) long

## Tension

26 sts x 34 rows measure 4in
(10cm) square over st-st using
3.25mm needles and DK yarn
before stuffing, or needles to give
correct tension.

## Abbreviations

See page 164

## How to make
## Duck-billed Platypus

### Body back
Using the long tail method and yarn A, cast on 28 sts.

**Rows 1 to 3:** Beg with a p row, work 3 rows in st-st.

**Row 4:** (K2, m1) 3 times, k16, (m1, k2) 3 times (34 sts).

**Rows 5 to 39:** Work 35 rows in st-st.

**Row 40:** (K4, k2tog) twice, k10, (k2tog, k4) twice (30 sts).

**Rows 41 to 45:** Work 5 rows in st-st.

**Row 46:** (K4, k2tog) twice, k6, (k2tog, k4) twice (26 sts).

**Rows 47 to 49:** Work 3 rows in st-st.

**Row 50:** (K3, k2tog) twice, k6, (k2tog, k3) twice (22 sts).

**Rows 51 to 53:** Work 3 rows in st-st.

**Row 54:** (K2, k2tog) twice, k6, (k2tog, k2) twice (18 sts).

**Row 55:** Purl.

**Row 56:** (K2, k2tog) twice, k2, (k2tog, k2) twice (14 sts).

**Row 57:** Purl.

Cast off.

### Tummy
Using the long tail method and yarn B, cast on 24 sts.

**Rows 1 to 3:** Beg with a p row, work 3 rows in st-st.

**Row 4:** (K2, m1) 3 times, k12, (m1, k2) 3 times (30 sts).

**Rows 5 to 39:** Work 35 rows in st-st.

**Row 40:** (K4, k2tog) twice, k6, (k2tog, k4) twice (26 sts).

**Rows 41 to 45:** Work 5 rows in st-st.

**Row 46:** (K4, k2tog) twice, k2, (k2tog, k4) twice (22 sts).

**Rows 47 to 49:** Work 3 rows in st-st.

**Row 50:** (K3, k2tog) twice, k2, (k2tog, k3) twice (18 sts).

**Rows 51 to 53:** Work 3 rows in st-st.

**Row 54:** K2, k2tog, k10, k2tog, k2 (16 sts).

**Row 55:** Purl.

**Row 56:** K2, k2tog, k8, k2tog, k2 (14 sts).

**Row 57:** Purl.

Cast off.

### Head
Using the long tail method and yarn A, cast on 50 sts.

**Rows 1 to 3:** Beg with a p row, work 3 rows in st-st.

**Row 4:** K11, (m1, k1) 4 times, k21, (m1, k1) 4 times, k10 (58 sts).

**Rows 5 to 19:** Work 15 rows in st-st.

**Row 20:** K8, (k2tog, k2) 4 times, k12, (k2tog, k2) 4 times, k6 (50 sts).

**Rows 21 to 23:** Work 3 rows in st-st.

**Rows 24 to 27:** Change to yarn C and k 2 rows then p 1 row then k 1 row.

**Rows 28 and 29:** K 1 row then p 1 row.

**Row 30:** K8, (k2tog) twice, k2, (k2tog) twice, k14, (k2tog) twice, k2, (k2tog) twice, k8 (42 sts).

**Row 31 and foll alt row:** Purl.

**Row 32:** K6, (k2tog) twice, k2, (k2tog) twice, k10, (k2tog) twice, k2, (k2tog) twice, k6 (34 sts).

**Row 34:** K4, (k2tog) twice, k2, (k2tog) twice, k6, (k2tog) twice, k2, (k2tog) twice, k4 (26 sts).

**Row 35:** Purl.

Cast off.

### Tail
Using the long tail method and yarn A, cast on 26 sts.

**Rows 1 to 3:** Beg with a p row, work 3 rows in st-st.

**Row 4:** K7, (m1, k4) 4 times, k3 (30 sts).

**Rows 5 to 7:** Work 3 rows in st-st.

**Row 8:** K5, (m1, k4) to last st, k1 (36 sts).

**Rows 9 to 21:** Work 13 rows in st-st.

**Row 22:** (K2tog, k4) to end (30 sts).

**Rows 23 to 27:** Work 5 rows in st-st.

**Row 28:** (K2tog, k3) to end (24 sts).

**Rows 29 to 33:** Work 5 rows in st-st.

**Row 34:** (K2tog, k2) to end (18 sts).

**Rows 35 to 39:** Work 5 rows in st-st.

**Row 40:** (K2tog, k1) to end (12 sts).

**Rows 41 to 43:** Work 3 rows in st-st.

**Row 44:** (K2tog) to end (6 sts).

Break yarn and thread through sts on needle, pull tight and secure by threading yarn a second time through sts.

### Bill
Using the long tail method and yarn C, cast on 26 sts.

**Row 1 and foll 3 alt rows:** Purl.

**Row 2:** K10, (m1, k2) 4 times, k8 (30 sts).

**Row 4:** K12, (m1, k2) 4 times, k10 (34 sts).

**Row 6:** K14, (m1, k2) 4 times, k12 (38 sts).

**Row 8:** K16, (m1, k2) 4 times, k14 (42 sts).

**Rows 9 and 10:** P 1 row then k 1 row.

**Rows 11 to 17:** Beg with a k row, rev st-st 7 rows.

**Rows 18 and 19:** K 1 row then p 1 row.

**Row 20:** K15, (k2tog, k1) twice, (k1, k2tog) twice, k15 (38 sts).
**Row 21 and foll 2 alt rows:** Purl.
**Row 22:** K13, (k2tog, k1) twice, (k1, k2tog) twice, k13 (34 sts).
**Row 24:** K11, (k2tog, k1) twice, (k1, k2tog) twice, k11 (30 sts).
**Row 26:** K9, (k2tog, k1) twice, (k1, k2tog) twice, k9 (26 sts).
Cast off pwise.

## Legs (make 4)

Using the long tail method and yarn A, cast on 24 sts.
**Rows 1 to 11:** Beg with a p row, work 11 rows in st-st.
**Row 12:** (K2tog, k8, k2tog) twice (20 sts).
**Row 13:** Purl.
**Row 14:** (K2tog, k6, k2tog) twice (16 sts).
**Row 15:** Purl.
Cast off.

## Flippers (make 4)

Using the long tail method and yarn C, cast on 12 sts.
**Row 1:** Purl.
**Row 2:** K1, (m1, k2) to last st, m1, k1 (18 sts).
**Rows 3 to 5:** Beg with a p row, work 3 rows in st-st.
**Rows 6 and 7:** Work 2 rows in g-st.
**Rows 8 to 11:** Beg with a k row, work 4 rows in st-st.
**Row 12:** (K2tog, k1) to end (12 sts).
**Row 13:** Purl.
Cast off.

## Making up Duck-billed Platypus

**Note:** Sew up all row-end seams on right side using mattress stitch one stitch in from the edge, unless otherwise stated; a one-stitch seam allowance has been allowed for this.

### Body back and tummy

Place wrong sides of body back and tummy together matching all edges and sew up side edges leaving neck and tail open. Stuff body pushing in stuffing through neck.

### Head

Sew up side edges of head and with this seam at centre of underneath, sew across cast-off stitches. Stuff head and pin and sew head to neck.

### Tail

Sew up side edges of tail and stuff. Sew tail to Platypus.

### Bill

Fold bill and on wrong side, oversew first and last loop of reverse stocking-stitch along inside edge of bill. Fold cast-on stitches in half and oversew. Fold cast-off stitches in half and oversew. Stuff bill and pin and sew to Platypus.

### Legs and flippers

Fold cast-off stitches of each leg in half and oversew. Sew up side edges of each leg and stuff legs. Sew open end of legs to body. Fold each flipper and oversew cast-on and cast-off stitches. Sew up one end, stuff flippers with tweezers or tip of scissors and sew up the other end. Sew flippers to ends of legs.

### Features

Using picture as a guide, embroider eyes in black making a chain stitch ring for each eye and fill in centre of eye with chain stitches (see page 163 for how to begin and fasten off invisibly for the embroidery).

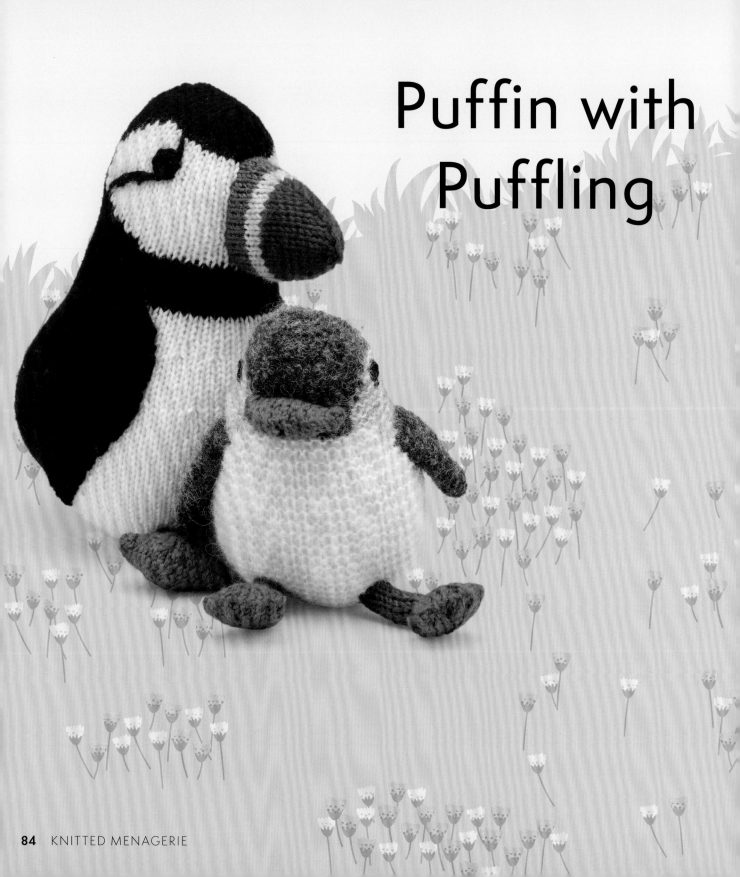

# Puffin with Puffling

# Information you'll need

## Materials
Any DK (US: light worsted) yarn
(amounts given are approximate)
**Yarn A** white (40g)
**Yarn B** black (40g) (2 separate balls
needed for intarsia)
**Yarn C** denim blue (5g)
**Yarn D** yellow (5g)
**Yarn E** red (5g)
**Yarn F** orange (10g)
**Yarn G** fluffy grey fashion yarn (10g)
(2 separate balls needed for intarsia)
**Yarn H** fluffy white fashion yarn (10g)
**Yarn I** fluffy dark grey fashion
yarn (10g)
Oddment of black for embroidery
1 pair of 3.25mm (UK10:US3) needles
5 knitters' bobbins
Knitters' pins and a blunt-ended needle
for sewing up
Acrylic toy stuffing

## Finished size
Puffin measures 8½in (21.5cm) high
Puffling measures 5½in (14cm) high

## Tension
26 sts x 34 rows measure 4in (10cm)
square over st-st using 3.25mm
needles and DK yarn before stuffing,
or needles to give correct tension.

## Abbreviations
See page 164

## Special abbreviation
**w1** – wrap 1 stitch: take yarn
between needles to opposite
side, slip one stitch pwise from
LH needle to RH needle and
take yarn back between the
needles to first side.

# How to make Puffin

## Body and head

Using the long tail method and yarn A, cast on 22 sts.

**Row 1 and foll 9 alt rows:** Purl.
**Row 2:** (K1, m1) twice, k8, m1, k2, m1, k8, (m1, k1) twice (28 sts).
**Row 4:** (K1, m1) twice, k11, m1, k2, m1, k11, (m1, k1) twice (34 sts).
**Row 6:** (K1, m1) twice, k14, m1, k2, m1, k14, (m1, k1) twice (40 sts).
**Row 8:** (K1, m1) twice, k17, m1, k2, m1, k17, (m1, k1) twice (46 sts).
**Row 10:** (K1, m1) twice, k20, m1, k2, m1, k20, (m1, k1) twice (52 sts).
**Row 12:** (K1, m1) twice, k13, (m1, k2) 12 times, k11, (m1, k1) twice (68 sts).
**Row 14:** (K1, m1) twice, k64, (m1, k1) twice (72 sts).
**Row 16:** (K1, m1) twice, k68, (m1, k1) twice (76 sts).
**Row 18:** (K1, m1) twice, k72, (m1, k1) twice (80 sts).
**Row 20:** (K1, m1) twice, k24, (m1, k4) 8 times, k20, (m1, k1) twice (92 sts).
Join on 2 balls of yarn B and rejoin yarn A and work in intarsia in blocks of colour, twisting yarn when changing colour to avoid a hole.
**Row 21:** Yarn B-p24, yarn A-p44, yarn B (second ball)-p24.
**Row 22:** Yarn B-k24, yarn A-k44, yarn B-k24.
**Row 23:** Yarn B-p25, yarn A-p42, yarn B-p25.
**Row 24:** Yarn B-k25, yarn A-k42, yarn B-k25.
**Row 25:** Yarn B-p26, yarn A-p40, yarn B-p26.
**Row 26:** Yarn B-k2tog, k24, yarn A-k40, yarn B-k24, k2tog (90 sts).
**Row 27:** Yarn B-p25, yarn A-p40, yarn B-p25.

**Row 28:** Yarn B-k2tog, k23, yarn A-k40, yarn B-k23, k2tog (88 sts).
**Row 29:** Yarn B-p24, yarn A-p40, yarn B-p24.
**Row 30:** Yarn B-k24, yarn A-p40, yarn B-k24.
**Row 31:** As row 29.
**Row 32:** Yarn B-k2tog, k22, yarn A-k40, yarn B-k22, k2tog (86 sts).
**Row 33:** Yarn B-p23, yarn A-p40, yarn B-p23.
**Row 34:** Yarn B-k23, yarn A-p40, yarn B-k23.
**Row 35:** As row 33.
**Row 36:** Yarn B-k2tog, k21, yarn A-k40, yarn B-k21, k2tog (84 sts).
**Row 37:** Yarn B-p22, yarn A-p40, yarn B-p22.
**Row 38:** Yarn B-k22, yarn A-p40, yarn B-k22.
**Row 39:** As row 37.
**Row 40:** Yarn B-k2tog, k20, yarn A-k4, (k2tog, k4) 6 times, yarn B-k20, k2tog (76 sts).
**Row 41:** Yarn B-p21, yarn A-p34, yarn B-p21.
**Row 42:** Yarn B-k21, yarn A-k34, yarn B-k21.
**Row 43:** As row 41.
**Row 44:** Yarn B-k2tog, k19, yarn A-k34, yarn B-k19, k2tog (74 sts).
**Row 45:** Yarn B-p20, yarn A-p34, yarn B-p20.
**Row 46:** Yarn B-k20, yarn A-k34, yarn B-k20.
**Row 47:** As row 45.
**Row 48:** Yarn B-k2tog, k18, yarn A-k2, (k2tog, k2) 8 times, yarn B-k18, k2tog (64 sts).
**Row 49:** Yarn B-p19, yarn A-p26, yarn B-p19.
**Row 50:** Yarn B-k19, yarn A-k26, yarn B-k19.
**Row 51:** As row 49.

**Row 52:** Yarn B-k2tog, k17, yarn A-k26, yarn B-k17, k2tog (62 sts).
**Row 53:** Yarn B-p18, yarn A-p26, yarn B-p18.
**Rows 54 and 55:** Cont with 1 ball of yarn B and k 1 row then p 1 row.
**Row 56:** K2tog, k to last 2 sts, k2tog (60 sts).
**Row 57:** Purl.
**Row 58:** K15, (k2tog, k2) 8 times, k13 (52 sts).
**Rows 59 to 61:** Beg with a p row, work 3 rows in st-st.
Join on yarn A and second ball of yarn B and work in intarsia in blocks of colour, twisting yarn when changing colour to avoid a hole, as foll:
**Row 62:** Yarn B-k15, yarn A-k22, yarn B (second ball)-k15.

**Row 63:** Yarn B-p13, yarn A-p26, yarn B-p13.
**Row 64:** Yarn B-k11, yarn A-k30, yarn B-k11.
**Row 65:** Yarn B-p9, yarn A-p34, yarn B-p9.
**Row 66:** Yarn B-k7, yarn A-k38, yarn B-k7.
**Row 67:** Yarn B-p7, yarn A-p38, yarn B-p7.
**Rows 68 to 73:** Rep rows 66 and 67, 3 times more.
**Row 74:** Yarn B-k8, yarn A-k36, yarn B-k8.
**Row 75:** Yarn B-p9, yarn A-p34, yarn B-p9.
**Row 76:** Yarn B-k10, yarn A-k32, yarn B-k10.
**Row 77:** Yarn B-p11, yarn A-p30, yarn B-p11.
**Row 78:** Yarn B-k12, yarn A-k28, yarn B-k12.
**Row 79:** Yarn B-p13, yarn A-p26, yarn B-p13.
Cont with 1 ball of yarn B and shape:
**Row 80:** K2tog, k to last 2 sts, k2tog (50 sts).

**Row 81 and foll 2 alt rows:** Purl.
**Row 82:** (K2tog, k2) twice, k9, (k2tog, k2) twice, (k2, k2tog) twice, k9, (k2, k2tog) twice (42 sts).
**Row 84:** (K2tog, k2) twice, k5, (k2tog, k2) twice, (k2, k2tog) twice, k5, (k2, k2tog) twice (34 sts).
**Row 86:** (K2tog) 3 times, k5, (k2tog) 6 times, k5, (k2tog) 3 times (22 sts).
**Row 87:** Purl.
Cast off.

## Beak
Using the long tail method and yarn C, cast on 31 sts.
**Rows 1 to 3:** Beg with a p row, work 3 rows in st-st.
**Row 4:** K14, k3tog, k14 (29 sts).
**Row 5:** Purl.
**Rows 6 and 7:** Change to yarn D and k 1 row then p 1 row.
**Row 8:** K13, k3tog, k13 (27 sts).
**Rows 9 to 11:** Change to yarn E and work 3 rows in st-st.
**Row 12:** K2tog, k10, k3tog, k10, k2tog (23 sts).
**Row 13 and foll 3 at rows:** Purl.
**Row 14:** K2tog, k8, k3tog, k8, k2tog (19 sts).
**Row 16:** K2tog, k6, k3tog, k6, k2tog (15 sts).
**Row 18:** K2tog, k4, k3tog, k4, k2tog (11 sts).
**Row 20:** K2tog, k2, k3tog, k2, k2tog (7 sts).
Thread yarn through sts on needle, pull tight and secure by threading yarn a second time through sts.

## Legs (make 2)
Using the long tail method and yarn F, cast on 20 sts.
**Rows 1 to 7:** Beg with a p row, work 7 rows in st-st.
Cast off.

## Feet (make 4 pieces)
Using the long tail method and yarn F, cast on 20 sts.
**Row 1:** Purl.
**Row 2:** K7, (k3tog) twice, k7 (16 sts).
**Shape toes**
**Row 3:** P10, w1 (see special abbreviation), turn.
**Row 4:** S1k, k4, w1, turn.
**Row 5:** S1p, p to end.
**Row 6:** (K2tog, k4, k2tog) twice (12 sts).
**Row 7:** Purl.
**Row 8:** K2tog, k to last 2 sts, k2tog (10 sts).
**Row 9:** Purl.
**Rows 10 and 11:** Rep rows 8 and 9 once (8 sts).
Cast off.

## Wings (make 2)
Using the long tail method and yarn B, cast on 10 sts and work in g-st.
**Rows 1 and 2:** Work 2 rows in g-st.
**Row 3:** K1, m1, k to last st, m1, k1 (12 sts).
**Row 4:** Knit.
**Rows 5 to 8:** Rep rows 3 and 4 twice more (16 sts).
**Rows 9 to 24:** Work 16 rows in g-st.
**Row 25:** K2tog, k to last 2 sts, k2tog (14 sts).
**Rows 26 to 28:** Work 3 rows in g-st.
**Rows 29 to 48:** Rep rows 25 to 28, 5 times more (4 sts).
**Row 49:** (K2tog) twice (2 sts).
Break yarn and thread through sts on needle, pull tight and secure by threading yarn a second time through sts.

## Making up Puffin

**Note:** Sew up all row-end seams on right side using mattress stitch one stitch in from the edge, unless otherwise stated; a one-stitch seam allowance has been allowed for this.

### Body and head
Fold cast-on stitches of body in half and oversew then fold cast-off stitches of head in half and oversew. Sew up side edges leaving a gap, stuff Puffin, pushing stuffing into tail and sew up gap.

### Beak
Sew up side edges of beak and stuff. Pin and sew beak to centre of head.

### Features
Using picture as a guide, mark position of eyes with two pins and embroider eyes in black making a chain stitch ring for each eye and fill in the centre with chain stitches. Embroider two lines on both sides of face using straight stitches (see page 163 for how to begin and fasten off invisibly for the embroidery).

### Legs and feet
Roll up legs from row ends to row ends and sew outside edge down. Place two pieces of feet together matching all edges and oversew cast-on stitches. Stuff feet and sew up row ends. Sew feet to legs and legs to Puffin.

### Wings
Sew wings to sides of Puffin.

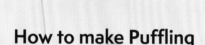

## How to make Puffling

**Note:** Before beg, wind 2 bobbins of yarn G and 3 bobbins of yarn I and reserve these.

### Body and head
Using the long tail method and yarn G, cast on 24 sts and work in g-st.
Join on yarn H and second ball of yarn G and work in intarsia in blocks of colour, twisting yarn on WS when changing colours to avoid a hole.
**Row 1 (RS):** Yarn G-k8, yarn H-k8, yarn G (second ball)-k8.
**Row 2:** As row 1.
**Row 3:** Yarn G-(k1, kfb) twice, k4, yarn H-(k1, kfb) twice, (kfb, k1) twice, yarn G-k4, (kfb, k1) twice, (32 sts).
**Row 4:** Yarn G-k10, yarn H-k12, yarn G-k10.
**Row 5:** Yarn G-(k1, kfb) twice, k6, yarn H-(k1, kfb) 3 times, (kfb, k1) 3 times, yarn G-k6, (kfb, k1) twice (42 sts).
**Row 6:** Yarn G-k12, yarn H-k18, yarn G-k12.
**Row 7:** Yarn G-(k1, kfb) twice, k8, yarn H-k3, (k1, kfb) 3 times, (kfb, k1) 3 times, k3, yarn G-k8, (kfb, k1) twice (52 sts).
**Row 8:** Yarn G-k14, yarn H-k24, yarn G-k14.
**Row 9:** Yarn G-(k1, kfb) twice, k10, yarn H-k6, (k1, kfb) 3 times, (kfb, k1) 3 times, k6, yarn G-k10, (kfb, k1) twice (62 sts).
**Row 10:** Yarn G-k16, yarn H-k30, yarn G-k16.
**Rows 11 to 24:** Rep row 10, 14 times more.
**Row 25:** Yarn G-k2tog, k14, yarn H-k30, yarn G-k14, k2tog (60 sts).
**Row 26:** Yarn G-k15, yarn H-k30, yarn G-k15.
**Rows 27 and 28:** Rep row 26 twice.
**Row 29:** Yarn G-k2tog, k13, yarn H-k30, yarn G-k13, k2tog (58 sts).
**Row 30:** Yarn G-k14, yarn H-k30, yarn G-k14.
**Row 31:** Yarn G-k15, yarn H-k28, yarn G-k15.
**Row 32:** As row 31.
**Row 33:** Yarn G-k2tog, k14, yarn H-k26, yarn G-k14, k2tog (56 sts).
**Row 34:** Yarn G-k15, yarn H-k26, yarn G-k15.
**Row 35:** Yarn G-k16, yarn H-k24, yarn G-k16.
**Row 36:** As row 35.
**Row 37:** Yarn G-k2tog, k15, yarn H-k1, (k2tog, k4) 3 times, k2tog, k1, yarn G-k15, k2tog (50 sts).
**Row 38:** Yarn G-k16, yarn H-k18, yarn G-k16.
**Row 39:** Yarn G-k17, yarn H-k16, yarn G-k17.
**Row 40:** As row 39.
**Row 41:** Yarn G-k2, (k2tog, k2) 4 times, yarn H-k2, (k2tog, k2) 3 times, yarn G-k2, (k2tog, k2) 4 times, (39 sts).
**Row 42:** Yarn G-k14, yarn H-k11, yarn G-k14.
Break off all colours and join on 3 bobbins in yarn I and 2 bobbins in yarn G, as foll:
**Row 43:** Yarn I (first bobbin)-k9, yarn G (first bobbin)-k6, yarn I (second bobbin)-k9, yarn G (second bobbin)-k6, yarn I (third bobbin)-k9.

**Row 44:** Yarn I-k9, yarn G-k6, yarn I-k9, yarn G-k6, yarn I-k9.
**Row 45:** Yarn I-k8, yarn G-k7, yarn I-k9, yarn G-k7, yarn I-k8.
**Row 46:** As row 45.
**Row 47:** Yarn I-k7, yarn G-k8, yarn I-k9, yarn G-k8, yarn I-k7.
**Row 48:** As row 47.
**Row 49:** Yarn I-k6, yarn G-k8, yarn I-k11, yarn G-k8, yarn I-k6.
**Row 50:** As row 49.
**Row 51:** Yarn I-k6, yarn G-k7, yarn I-k13, yarn G-k7, yarn I-k6.
**Row 52:** As row 51.
**Row 53:** Yarn I-k7, yarn G-k5, yarn I-k15, yarn G-k5, yarn I-k7.
**Row 54:** As row 53.
**Rows 55 and 56:** Cont with 1 ball of yarn I and work 2 rows in g-st.
**Row 57:** K2tog, k to last 2 sts, k2tog (37 sts).
**Row 58 and foll 3 alt rows:** Knit.
**Row 59:** (K2tog, k4) 3 times, k1, (k4, k2tog) 3 times, (31 sts).
**Row 61:** (K2tog, k3) 3 times, k1, (k3, k2tog) 3 times (25 sts).
**Row 63:** (K2tog, k2) 3 times, k1, (k2, k2tog) 3 times (19 sts).
**Row 65:** K1, (k2tog, k1) to end (13 sts).
**Row 66:** K1, (k2tog, k1) to end (9 sts).
Break yarn and thread through sts on needle, pull tight and secure by threading yarn a second time through sts.

## Legs (make 2)
Using the long tail method and yarn F, cast on 14 sts.
**Rows 1 to 9:** Beg with a p row, work 9 rows in st-st.
Cast off.

## Feet (make 4 pieces)
Using the long tail method and yarn F, cast on 14 sts.
**Row 1 and foll 3 alt rows:** Purl.
**Row 2:** K4, (k3tog) twice, k4 (10 sts).
**Row 4:** K4, k2tog, k4 (9 sts).
**Row 6:** K3, (k3tog) k3 (7 sts).
**Row 8:** K2tog, k3, k2tog (5 sts).
**Row 9:** Purl.
Cast off.

## Beak (make 2 pieces)
Using the long tail method and yarn F, cast on 14 sts.
**Row 1:** Purl.
**Row 2:** K2tog, k to last 2 sts, k2tog (12 sts).
**Row 3:** P2tog, p to last 2 sts, p2tog (10 sts).
**Rows 4 to 6:** Rep rows 2 and 3 once, then row 2 once (4 sts).
**Row 7:** Purl.
Break yarn and thread through sts on needle, pull tight and secure by threading yarn a second time through sts.

## Wings (make 2)
Using the long tail method and yarn I, cast on 12 sts and work in g-st.
**Rows 1 and 2:** Work 2 rows in g-st.
**Row 3:** (Kfb, k4, kfb) twice (16 sts).
**Row 4:** Knit.
**Row 5:** Kfb, k to last 2 sts, kfb (18 sts).
**Rows 6 to 12:** Work 7 rows in g-st.
**Row 13:** K2tog, k to last 2 sts, k2tog (16 sts).
**Rows 14 and 15:** Rep row 13 twice more (12 sts).
**Rows 16 to 24:** Work 9 rows in g-st.
**Row 25:** (K2tog) to end (6 sts).
Break yarn and thread through sts on needle, pull tight and secure by threading yarn a second time through sts.

# Making up Puffling

**Note:** Sew up all row-end seams on right side using mattress stitch one stitch in from the edge, unless otherwise stated; a one-stitch seam allowance has been allowed for this.

## Body and head
Fold cast-on stitches of body in half and oversew. Sew up side edges leaving a gap, stuff Puffling, pushing stuffing into tail and sew up gap.

## Legs and feet
Roll up legs from row ends to row ends and sew outside edge down. Place two pieces of feet together matching all edges and oversew cast-on stitches. Stuff feet and sew up row ends. Sew feet to legs and legs to Puffling.

## Beak
Place two pieces of beak together matching all edges, oversew row ends and stuff. Pin and sew beak to centre front of head.

## Wings
Fold cast-on stitches of wings in half and oversew. Sew up side edges and sew wings to sides of Puffling.

## Features
Using picture as a guide, mark position of eyes with two pins and embroider eyes in black making a circle of chain stitches for each eye and fill in the centre with chain stitches (see page 163 for how to begin and fasten off invisibly for the embroidery).

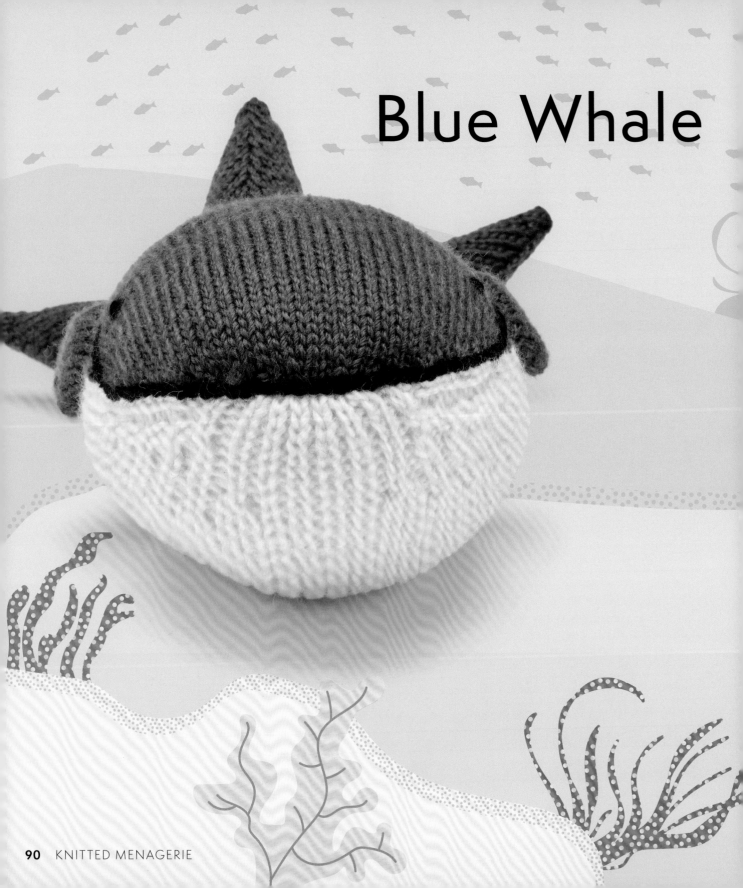

# Blue Whale

# Information you'll need

## Materials
Any DK (US: light worsted) yarn
(amounts given are approximate)
**Yarn A** denim blue (50g)
**Yarn B** white (40g)
Oddment of black for embroidery
1 pair of 3.25mm (UK10:US3) needles
Knitters' pins and a blunt-ended needle for sewing up
Tweezers (optional)
Acrylic toy stuffing

## Finished size
Blue Whale measures 12in (30.5cm) long

## Tension
26 sts x 34 rows measure 4in (10cm)
square over st-st using 3.25mm
needles and DK yarn before
stuffing, or needles to
give correct tension.

## Abbreviations
See page 164

# How to make Blue Whale

## Body and head

Using the long tail method and yarn A, cast on 12 sts.

**Rows 1 to 3:** Beg with a p row, work 3 rows in st-st.

**Row 4:** K1, m1, k to last st, m1, k1 (14 sts).

**Rows 5 and 6:** P 1 row then k 1 row.

**Row 7:** P1, m1, p to last st, m1, p1 (16 sts).

**Rows 8 and 9:** K 1 row then p 1 row.

**Rows 10 to 45:** Rep rows 4 to 9, 6 times more (40 sts).

**Rows 46 to 69:** Work 24 rows in st-st.

**Row 70:** K2tog, k to last 2 sts, k2tog (38 sts).

**Row 71:** Purl.

**Rows 72 to 87:** Rep rows 70 and 71, 8 times more (22 sts).

**Row 88:** K2tog, k to last 2 sts, k2tog (20 sts).

**Row 89:** P2tog, p to last 2 sts, p2tog (18 sts).

**Rows 90 and 91:** Rep rows 88 and 89 once (14 sts).

**Row 92:** K2tog, (k2, k2tog) to end (10 sts).

**Row 93:** P2tog, p to last 2 sts, p2tog (8 sts). Cast off.

## Tummy

Using the long tail method and yarn A, cast on 12 sts.

**Rows 1 to 3:** Beg with a p row, work 3 rows in st-st.

**Row 4:** K1, m1, k to last st, m1, k1 (14 sts).

**Rows 5 to 36:** Rep rows 1 to 4, 8 times more (30 sts).

**Rows 37 to 42:** Work 6 rows in st-st, ending on a k row.

**Row 43:** Change to yarn B and p 1 row.

**Row 44:** P1, (kfb) to last 2 sts, k1, p1 (57 sts).

**Row 45:** K1, (p1, k1) to end (this row sets the rib).

**Rows 46 to 73:** Cont in rib as set for 28 rows.

**Row 74:** (P1, k1, p1, k3tog) twice, p1, (k1, p1) 16 times, (k3tog, p1, k1, p1) twice (49 sts).

**Rows 75 to 77:** Work 3 rows in rib.

**Row 78:** (P1, k1, p1, k3tog) twice, p1, (k1, p1) 12 times, (k3tog, p1, k1 p1) twice (41 sts).

**Rows 79 to 81:** Work 3 rows in rib.

**Row 82:** (P1, k1, p1, k3tog) twice, p1, (k1, p1) 8 times, (k3tog, p1, k1 p1) twice (33 sts).

**Rows 83 to 85:** Work 3 rows in rib.

**Row 86:** (P1, k1, p1, k3tog) twice, p1, (k1, p1) 4 times, (k3tog, p1, k1, p1) twice (25 sts).

**Rows 87 to 89:** Work 3 rows in rib.

**Row 90:** P1, k1, p1, k3tog, p1, (k1, p1) 6 times, k3tog, p1, k1 p1 (21 sts).

**Row 91 and foll 2 alt rows:** Work 1 row in rib.

**Row 92:** P2tog, k2tog, rib to last 4 sts, k2tog, p2tog (17 sts).

**Row 94:** K2tog, rib to last 2 sts, k2tog (15 sts).

**Row 96:** K1, (k2tog) to end (8 sts). Cast off pwise.

## Tail (make 2 pieces)

Using the long tail method and yarn A, cast on 16 sts.

**Rows 1 to 3:** Beg with a p row, work 3 rows in st-st.

**Row 4:** K2 (m1, k1) 6 times, (k1 m1) 6 times, k2 (28 sts).

**Rows 5 to 15:** Beg with a p row, work 11 rows in st-st.

**Row 16:** K13, k2tog, k13 (27 sts).

**Row 17 and foll 10 alt rows:** Purl.

**Row 18:** K12, k3tog, k12 (25 sts).

**Row 20:** K11, k3tog, k11 (23 sts).

**Row 22:** K10, k3tog, k10 (21 sts).

**Row 24:** K9, k3tog, k9 (19 sts).

**Row 26:** K8, k3tog, k8 (17 sts).

**Row 28:** K7, k3tog, k7 (15 sts).

**Row 30:** K6, k3tog, k6 (13 sts).

**Row 32:** K5, k3tog, k5 (11 sts).

**Row 34:** K4, k3tog, k4 (9 sts).
**Row 36:** K3, k3tog, k3 (7 sts).
**Row 38:** K2, k3tog, k2 (5 sts).
Break yarn and thread through sts on needle, pull tight and secure by threading yarn a second time through sts.

## Fins (make 2)
Using the long tail method and yarn A, cast on 18 sts.
**Rows 1 to 11:** Beg with a p row, work 11 rows in st-st.
**Row 12:** K8, k2tog, k8 (17 sts).
**Row 13 and foll 4 alt rows:** Purl.
**Row 14:** K7, k3tog, k7 (15 sts).
**Row 16:** K6, k3tog, k6 (13 sts).
**Row 18:** K5, k3tog, k5 (11 sts).
**Row 20:** K4, k3tog, k4 (9 sts).
**Row 22:** K3, k3tog, k3 (7 sts).
Break yarn and thread through sts on needle, pull tight and secure by threading yarn a second time through sts.

## Dorsal fin
Using the long tail method and yarn A, cast on 26 sts.
**Rows 1 to 3:** Beg with a p row, work 3 rows in st-st.
**Row 4:** K12, k2tog, k12 (25 sts).
**Row 5 and foll 6 alt rows:** Purl.
**Row 6:** K11, k3tog, k11 (23 sts).
**Row 8:** K2tog, k8, k3tog, k8, k2tog (19 sts).
**Row 10:** K8, k3tog, k8 (17 sts).
**Row 12:** K2tog, k5, k3tog, k5, k2tog (13 sts).
**Row 14:** K5, k3tog, k5 (11 sts).
**Row 16:** K2tog, k2, k3tog, k2, k2tog (7 sts).
**Row 18:** K2, k3tog, k2 (5 sts).
Break yarn and thread through sts on needle, pull tight and secure by threading yarn a second time through sts.

# Making up Blue Whale

**Note:** Sew up all row-end seams on right side using mattress stitch one stitch in from the edge, unless otherwise stated; a one-stitch seam allowance has been allowed for this.

## Body, head and tummy
Place wrong sides of body and tummy together, matching all edges and pin around outside edge. Sew up outside edge leaving a gap, stuff and sew up gap.

## Tail
Sew up side edges of both pieces of tail and stuff, pushing stuffing into tip with tweezers or tip of scissors. Fold cast-on stitches of both pieces of tail in half and oversew, then sew cast-on stitches of two halves of tail together. Sew tail to Whale.

## Fins
Fold cast-on stitches of fins in half and sew up. Sew up side edges and sew fins to Whale.

## Dorsal fin
Sew up side edges of dorsal fin and stuff, pushing stuffing into tip with tweezers or tip of scissors. Pin and sew dorsal fin to the Whale.

## Features
Using picture as a guide, embroider mouth in black using chain stitch. Mark position of eyes with two pins and embroider eyes in black making a vertical chain stitch for each eye, then a second chain stitch on top of first (see page 163 for how to begin and fasten off invisibly for the embroidery).

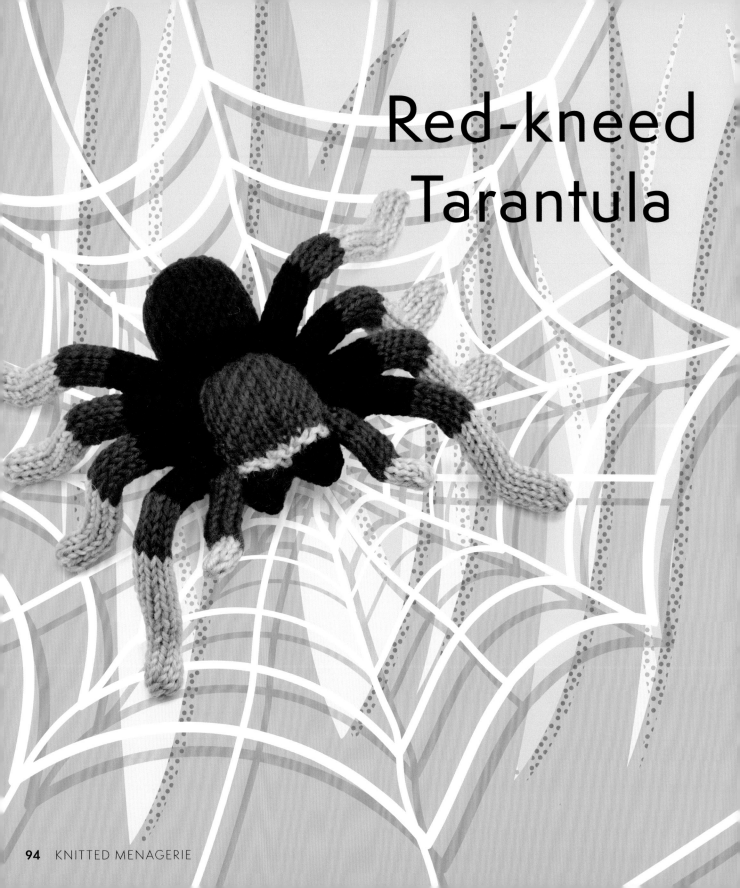

# Red-kneed Tarantula

# Information you'll need

## Materials
Any DK (US: light worsted) yarn
(amounts given are approximate)
**Yarn A** red (10g)
**Yarn B** cream (10g)
**Yarn C** brown (5g)
**Yarn D** black (5g)
1 pair of 3.25mm (UK10:US3) needles
A blunt-ended needle for sewing up
Acrylic toy stuffing
9 chenille stems

## Finished size
Tarantula measures 7in (18cm) across

## Tension
26 sts x 34 rows measure 4in (10cm) square
over st-st using 3.25mm needles and
DK yarn before stuffing, or needles
to give correct tension.

## Abbreviations
See page 164

# How to make Red-kneed Tarantula

## Body

### Front body segment

Using the long tail method and yarn A, cast on 12 sts.

**Row 1 and foll alt row:** Purl.

**Row 2:** *(K1, m1) twice, k2 (m1, k1) twice; rep from * once (20 sts).

**Row 4:** *(K2, m1) twice, k2 (m1, k2) twice; rep from * once (28 sts).

**Rows 5 to 11:** Beg with a p row, work 7 rows in st-st.**

**Row 12:** *(K1, k2tog) twice, k2, (k2tog, k1) twice; rep from * once (20 sts).

**Row 13:** Purl.

**Rows 14 and 15:** Change to yarn B and work 2 rows in g-st.

Cont in yarn C and patt, as foll:

**Row 16:** K10, turn and work on these 10 sts.

**Rows 17 to 19:** Beg with a p row, work 3 rows in st-st.

**Row 20:** (K2tog) to end (5 sts).

Break yarn and thread through sts on needle, pull tight and secure by threading yarn a second time through sts.

**Row 21:** Rejoin yarn C to rem sts and k to end (10 sts).

**Rows 22 and 25:** Rep from row 17 to row 20 once.

Break yarn and thread through sts on needle, pull tight and secure by threading yarn a second time through sts.

### Rear body segment

Using the long tail method and yarn C, cast on 12 sts.

**Rows 1 to 11:** Work from beg to **, as for front body segment.

**Row 12:** (K2tog, k2) to end (21 sts).

**Row 13:** Purl.

**Rows 14 and 15:** Change to yarn D and k 1 row then p 1 row.

**Row 16:** (K2tog, k1) to end (14 sts).

**Row 17:** Purl.

Cast off.

## Antennae (make 2)

Using the long tail method and yarn A, cast on 8 sts.

**Rows 1 to 9:** Beg with a p row, work 9 rows in st-st.

**Rows 10 to 13:** Change to yarn B and work 4 rows in st-st.

Break yarn and thread through sts on needle, pull tight and secure by threading yarn a second time through sts.

## Long legs (make 4)

Using the long tail method and yarn D, cast on 10 sts.

**Rows 1 to 9:** Beg with a p row, work 9 rows in st-st.

**Rows 10 to 15:** Change to yarn A and work 6 rows in st-st.

**Rows 16 to 31:** Change to yarn B and work 16 rows in st-st.

Break yarn and thread through sts on needle, pull tight and secure by threading yarn a second time through sts.

## Short legs (make 4)

Using the long tail method and yarn D, cast on 10 sts.

**Rows 1 to 7:** Beg with a p row, work 7 rows in st-st.

**Rows 8 to 13:** Change to yarn A and work 6 rows in st-st.

**Rows 14 to 25:** Change to yarn B and work 12 rows in st-st.

Break yarn and thread through sts on needle, pull tight and secure by threading yarn a second time through sts.

# Making up
# Red-kneed Tarantula

**Note:** Sew up all row-end seams on right side using mattress stitch one stitch in from the edge, unless otherwise stated; a one-stitch seam allowance has been allowed for this.

## Body

Sew up both sets of row-ends at front of front body segment, then sew up row ends of underneath and stuff. Sew across cast-on stitches. Sew up row ends of rear body segment and with seam at centre of underneath, sew across cast-on stitches. Stuff and sew cast-off stitches to rear of front body segment.

## Antennae

Place a chenille stem along wrong side of antennae and sew up row ends along length of antennae, enclosing chenille stem inside. Cut chenille stem to length of antennae and sew antennae to front body segment at each side. Using picture as a guide, bend antennae.

## Legs

Fold a chenille stem in half and place fold into wrong side of stitches pulled tight on a thread. Sew up row ends along length of legs, enclosing chenille stems inside. Cut chenille stems to length of legs and sew legs to front body segment, placing a long leg at front and back of each side and two short legs in between. Bend legs round and bend tips of legs out.

# Blue Jay

# Information you'll need

## Materials
Any DK (US: light worsted) yarn
(amounts given are approximate)
**Yarn A** white (10g)
**Yarn B** pale blue (5g)
**Yarn C** black (5g)
**Yarn D** medium blue (15g)
**Yarn E** grey (5g)
Oddment of black for embroidery
1 pair of 3.25mm (UK10:US3) needles
Stitch holder
Knitters' pins and a blunt-ended needle for sewing up
Tweezers (optional)
Acrylic toy stuffing
2 straight wooden lollipop sticks
1 chenille stem

## Finished size
Blue Jay measures 9in (23cm) high

## Tension
26 sts x 34 rows measure 4in (10cm) square over st-st
using 3.25mm needles and DK yarn before stuffing, or
needles to give correct tension.

## Abbreviations
See page 164

## Special abbreviation
**w1** – wrap 1 stitch: take yarn between needles to
opposite side, slip one stitch pwise from LH needle to
RH needle and take yarn back between the needles
to first side.

# How to make Blue Jay

## Body and head

Using the long tail method and yarn A, cast on 18 sts and place a marker at centre of cast-on edge.

**Row 1 and foll 2 alt rows:** Purl.

**Row 2:** K2, (m1, k2) to end (26 sts).

**Row 4:** *(K2, m1) twice, k5, (m1, k2) twice; rep from * once (34 sts).

**Row 6:** *(K2, m1) twice, k9, (m1, k2) twice; rep from * once (42 sts).

**Row 7:** Purl.

**Row 8:** K34, w1 (see special abbreviation), turn.

**Row 9:** S1p, p26, w1, turn.

**Row 10:** S1k, k to end.

**Rows 11 to 13:** Work 3 rows in st-st.

**Rows 14 to 37:** Rep rows 8 to 13, 4 times more.

Join on yarn B and shape, as foll:

**Row 38:** K10, turn.

**Row 39:** S1p, p to end.

**Row 40:** K8, turn.

**Row 41:** S1p, p to end.

**Row 42:** K6, turn.

**Row 43:** S1p, p to end.

**Row 44:** K4, turn.

**Row 45:** S1p, p to end.

**Row 46:** Slip all stitches pwise from LH needle to RH needle. Rejoin yarn B and shape, as foll:

**Row 47:** P10, turn.

**Row 48:** S1k, k to end.

**Row 49:** P8, turn.

**Row 50:** S1k, k to end.

**Row 51:** P6, turn.

**Row 52:** S1k, k to end.

**Row 53:** P4, turn.

**Row 54:** S1k, k to end.

Join on yarn C and dec, as foll:

**Row 55:** P9, (p2tog, p2) 3 times, (p2, p2tog) 3 times, p9 (36 sts).

**Row 56:** K11, w1, turn.

**Row 57:** S1p, p to end.

**Row 58:** Knit.

**Row 59:** P11, w1, turn.

**Row 60:** S1k, k to end.

Change to yarn B and dec, as foll:

**Row 61:** P14, (p2tog) 4 times, p14 (32 sts).

**Rows 62 to 71:** Work 10 rows in st-st.

**Row 72:** (K2tog, k2) to end (24 sts).

**Row 73 and foll alt row:** Purl.

**Row 74:** (K2tog, k1) to end (16 sts).

**Row 76:** (K2tog) to end (8 sts).

Break yarn and thread yarn through sts on needle, pull tight and secure by threading yarn a second time through sts.

## Tail

Using the long tail method and yarn D, cast on 12 sts.

**Rows 1 to 13:** Beg with a p row, work 13 rows in st-st.

**Rows 14 and 15:** Using the knitting-on method, cast on 6 sts at beg of next 2 rows (24 sts).

**Rows 16 and 17:** Work 2 rows in st-st.

**Row 18:** K12, place rem sts onto stitch holder, turn and work on these 12 sts.

**\*\*Row 19:** Purl.

Join on yarn C and work in yarn C and yarn D, carrying yarn loosely up side of work, as foll:

**Rows 20 and 21:** Yarn C-work 2 rows in st-st.

**Rows 22 to 25:** Yarn D-work 4 rows in st-st.

**Rows 26 and 27:** Yarn C-work 2 rows in st-st.

**Rows 28 to 39:** Rep rows 22 to 27 twice more.

**Rows 40 and 41:** Cont in yarn D and work 2 rows in st-st.

**Row 42:** K2tog, k2, (k2tog) twice, k2, k2tog (8 sts).

**Row 43:** Purl.

Break yarn and thread through sts on needle, pull tight and secure by threading yarn a second time through sts.

**Row 44:** Replace stitches on stitch holder onto needle, rejoin yarn D and k to end (12 sts).

**Rows 45 to 69:** Work from \*\* to end.

## Wings

Using the long tail method and yarn D, cast on 56 sts.

**Row 1 and foll 3 alt rows:** Purl.

**Row 2:** (K13, m1, k2, m1, k13) twice (60 sts).

**Row 4:** (K14, m1, k2, m1, k14) twice (64 sts).

**Row 6:** (K15, m1, k2, m1, k15) twice (68 sts).

**Row 8:** (K16, m1, k2, m1, k16) twice (72 sts).

**Rows 9 to 13:** Work 5 rows in st-st.

**Rows 14 and 15:** Join on yarn A, work 2 rows in st-st.

**Row 16:** *K16, k2tog tbl, k2tog, k16; rep from * once (68 sts).

**Row 17:** Purl.

Join on yarn C and dec, as foll:

**Row 18:** *K2tog, k13, k2tog tbl, k2tog, k13, k2tog tbl; rep from * once (60 sts).

**Row 19:** Purl.

Cont in yarn D and dec, as foll:

**Row 20:** *K13, k2tog tbl, k2tog, k13; rep from * once (56 sts).

**Row 21 and foll alt row:** Purl.

**Row 22:** *K2tog, k10, k2tog tbl, k2tog, k10, k2tog tbl; rep from * once (48 sts).

**Row 24:** *K10, k2tog tbl, k2tog, k10; rep from * once (44 sts).

**Row 25:** Purl.

Rejoin yarn A and dec, as foll:

**Row 26:** K2tog, k7, k2tog tbl, k2tog, k7, k2tog tbl, turn and work on these 18 sts.
**Rows 27 to 29:** Work 3 rows in st-st. Rejoin yarn C and dec, as foll:
**Row 30:** K2tog, k5, k2tog tbl, k2tog, k5, k2tog tbl (14 sts).
**Row 31 and foll alt row:** Purl.
**Row 32:** K2tog, k3, k2tog tbl, k2tog, k3, k2tog tbl (10 sts).
**Row 34:** (K2tog) to end (5 sts).
Break yarn and thread through sts on needle, pull tight and secure by threading yarn a second time through sts.
**Rows 35 to 43:** Rejoin yarn A to rem sts and work from ** to end once.

## Beak

Using the long tail method and yarn C, cast on 8 sts.
**Rows 1 to 5:** Beg with a p row, work 5 rows in st-st.
**Row 6:** K3, k2tog, k3 (7 sts).
**Row 7:** Purl.
Break yarn and thread through sts on needle, pull tight and secure by threading yarn a second time through sts.

## Crest

Using the long tail method and yarn D, cast on 6 sts.
**Row 1 and foll 2 alt rows:** Purl.
**Row 2:** (K1, m1, k1, m1, k1) twice (10 sts).
**Row 4:** (K1, m1) 3 times, k4, (m1, k1) 3 times (16 sts).
**Row 6:** (K1, m1) 3 times, k10, (m1, k1) 3 times (22 sts).
**Rows 7 to 13:** Work 7 rows in st-st.
**Row 14:** K2, (k2tog) twice, k10, (k2tog) twice, k2 (18 sts).
**Row 15 and foll 2 alt rows:** Purl.
**Row 16:** K2, (k2tog) twice, k6, (k2tog) twice, k2 (14 sts).
**Row 18:** (K2tog) twice, k6, (k2tog) twice (10 sts).

**Row 20:** (K2tog) twice, k2, (k2tog) twice (6 sts).
**Row 21:** (P2tog) to end (3 sts).
Break yarn and thread through sts on needle, pull tight and secure by threading yarn a second time through sts.

## Centre and back claws (make 2)

Using the long tail method and yarn E, cast on 7 sts.
**Rows 1 to 11:** Beg with a p row, work 11 rows in st-st.
Break yarn and thread through sts on needle, pull tight and secure by threading yarn a second time through sts.

## Side claws (make 4)

Using the long tail method and yarn E, cast on 7 sts.
**Rows 1 to 4:** Beg with a p row, work 4 rows in st-st, ending with a k row.
**Row 5:** P2tog, p3, p2tog (5 sts).
**Row 6:** K2tog, k1, k2tog (3 sts).
Break yarn and thread through sts on needle, pull tight and secure by threading yarn a second time through sts.

# Making up Blue Jay

**Note:** Sew up all row-end seams on right side using mattress stitch one stitch in from the edge, unless otherwise stated; a one-stitch seam allowance has been allowed for this.

## Body and head

Sew up side edges of body and head leaving a gap, bring marker and seam together and sew across cast-on stitches. Stuff head then body and sew up gap.

## Tail

Fold cast-off stitches of both halves of tail in half and oversew. Sew up row ends of tail pieces and place a lollipop stick, cut to 3½in (9cm) into both sides. Pin and sew tail on, sewing edges of patch to lower back.

## Wings

Bring side edges of wings together and oversew and sew round points. With seam at centre of inside edge, sew across cast-on stitches. Sew cast-on stitches to neck of Blue Jay and sew around all edges.

## Beak

Sew up side edges of beak and stuff beak with tweezers or tip of scissors. Sew beak to head.

## Crest

Sew up side edges of crest and with this seam at centre of inside edge, oversew cast-on stitches. Pin and sew crest to head.

## Features

Using picture as a guide, mark position of eyes with two pins and embroider eyes in black making a vertical chain stitch for each eye, then a second chain stitch on top of first. Embroider markings on face each side of eyes using satin stitch (see page 163 for how to begin and fasten off invisibly).

## Claws

Cut chenille stem in half. Take each half and fold in half and place each fold into stitches pulled tight on a thread of centre and back claw. Sew up side edges enclosing chenille stems inside, cut chenille stems to length of claws and gather round cast-on stitches. Sew up straight row ends of side claws and stuff with tweezers or tip of scissors. Sew side claws to centre claws, one each side. Sew claws to underneath of Blue Jay.

# Bumblebee

# Information you'll need

## Materials
Any DK (US: light worsted) yarn
(amounts given are approximate)
**Yarn A** black (40g)
**Yarn B** yellow (15g)
**Yarn C** white (10g)
**Yarn D** beige (10g)
1 pair of 3.25mm (UK10:US3) needles
A blunt-ended needle for sewing up
Acrylic toy stuffing
13 black chenille stems
Thick cardboard

## Finished size
Bumblebee measures 8¾in (22cm) long

## Tension
26 sts x 34 rows measure 4in (10cm) square over st-st
using 3.25mm needles and DK yarn before stuffing,
or needles to give correct tension.

## Abbreviations
See page 164

# How to make Bumblebee

## Head and body

Using the long tail method and yarn A, cast on 24 sts.
Place a marker at centre of cast-on edge.
**Row 1:** Purl.
**Row 2:** *K4, (m1, k1) twice, (k1, m1) twice, k4; rep from * once (32 sts).
**Rows 3 to 9:** Beg with a p row, work 7 rows in st-st.
Change to yarn B, cont in g-st and inc, as foll:
**Row 10:** *K4, (m1, k1) 4 times, (k1, m1) 4 times, k4; rep from * once (48 sts).
**Rows 11 to 21:** Work 11 rows in g-st.
**Rows 22 to 29:** Change to yarn A and work 8 rows in g-st.
**Row 30:** *K5, (k2tog, k2) 4 times, k3; rep from * once (40 sts).
**Row 31:** Knit.
**Row 32:** *K6, (k2tog) 4 times, k6; rep from * once (32 sts).
**Row 33:** (K1 tbl) to end.
**Row 34 and foll 2 alt rows:** Knit.
**Row 35:** *K5, (m1, k2) 4 times, k3; rep from * once (40 sts).
**Row 37:** *K7, (m1, k2) 4 times, k5; rep from * once (48 sts).
**Row 39:** *K9, (m1, k2) 4 times, k7; rep from * once (56 sts).
**Rows 40 to 47:** Work 8 rows in g-st.
**Rows 48 to 59:** Change to yarn B and work 12 rows in g-st.
**Rows 60 to 71:** Change to yarn A and work 12 rows in g-st.
**Rows 72 to 81:** Change to yarn C and work 10 rows in g-st.
**Row 82:** (K2tog, k5) to end (48 sts).
**Rows 83 to 85:** Work 3 rows in g-st.
**Row 86:** (K2tog, k4) to end (40 sts).
**Row 87 and foll 3 alt rows:** Knit.
**Row 88:** (K2tog, k3) to end (32 sts).

**Row 90:** (K2tog, k2) to end (24 sts).
**Row 92:** (K2tog, k1) to end (16 sts).
**Row 94:** (K2tog) to end (8 sts).
Break yarn and thread through sts on needle, pull tight and secure by threading yarn a second time through sts.

## Forelegs (make 2)

Using the long tail method and yarn A, cast on 9 sts.
**Rows 1 to 9:** Beg with a p row, work 9 rows in st-st.
**Rows 10 and 11:** Yarn B-work 2 rows in g-st.
**Rows 12 to 17:** Yarn A-work 6 rows in st-st.
**Rows 18 and 19:** Yarn B-work 2 rows in g-st.
Change to yarn A and dec, as foll:
**Row 20:** (K2tog, k1) to end (6 sts).
**Rows 21 to 27:** Beg with a p row, work 7 rows in st-st.
Break yarn and thread through sts on needle, pull tight and secure by threading yarn a second time through sts.

## Hind legs (make 4)

Using the long tail method and yarn A, cast on 9 sts.
**Rows 1 to 19:** Beg with a p row, work 19 rows in st-st.
**Rows 20 and 21:** Yarn B-work 2 rows in g-st.
**Rows 22 to 31:** Yarn A-work 10 rows in st-st.
**Rows 32 and 33:** Yarn B-work 2 rows in g-st.

Change to yarn A and dec:
**Row 34:** (K2tog, k1) to end (6 sts).
**Rows 35 to 41:** Beg with a p row, work 7 rows in st-st.
Break yarn and thread through sts on needle, pull tight and secure by threading yarn a second time through sts.

## Wings (make 2)

Using the long tail method and yarn D, cast on 10 sts.
**Rows 1 to 3:** Beg with a p row, work 3 rows in st-st.
**Row 4:** K1, m1, k to last st, m1, k1 (12 sts).
**Row 5:** Purl.
**Row 6:** (K1, m1, k4, m1, k1) twice (16 sts).
**Rows 7 to 9:** Work 3 rows in st-st.
**Row 10:** (K1, m1, k6, m1, k1) twice (20 sts).
**Rows 11 to 13:** Work 3 rows in st-st.
**Row 14:** (K1, m1, k8, m1, k1) twice (24 sts).
**Rows 15 to 17:** Work 3 rows in st-st.
**Row 18:** (K1, m1, k10, m1, k1) twice (28 sts).
**Rows 19 to 21:** Work 3 rows in st-st.
**Row 22:** (K1, m1, k12, m1, k1) twice (32 sts).
**Rows 23 to 25:** Work 3 rows in st-st.
**Row 26:** (K1, m1, k14, m1, k1) twice (36 sts).
**Rows 27 to 29:** Work 3 rows in st-st.
**Row 30:** (K1, m1, k16, m1, k1) twice (40 sts).
**Rows 31 to 35:** Work 5 rows in st-st.
**Row 36:** (K2tog, k16, k2tog tbl) twice (36 sts).
**Row 37 and foll 3 alt rows:** Purl.
**Row 38:** (K2tog, k14, k2tog tbl) twice (32 sts).

**Row 40:** (K2tog, k12, k2tog tbl) twice (28 sts).
**Row 42:** (K2tog, k10, k2tog tbl) twice (24 sts).
**Row 44:** (K2tog, k1, k2tog, k2, k2tog, k1, k2tog tbl) twice (16 sts).
Cast off pwise.

## Antennae (make 2)

Using the long tail method and yarn A, cast on 6 sts.
**Rows 1 to 13:** Beg with a p row, work 13 rows in st-st.
Break yarn and thread through sts on needle, pull tight and secure by threading yarn a second time through sts.

## Eyes (make 2)

Using the long tail method and yarn A, cast on 5 sts.
**Row 1:** Purl.
**Row 2:** K1, m1, k3, m1, k1 (7 sts).
**Rows 3 to 5:** Work 3 rows in st-st.
**Row 6:** K1, (k2tog, k1) twice (5 sts).
Break yarn and thread through sts on needle, pull tight and secure by threading yarn a second time through sts.

# Making up Bumblebee

**Note:** Sew up all row-end seams on right side using mattress stitch one stitch in from the edge, unless otherwise stated; a one-stitch seam allowance has been allowed for this.

## Head and body

Sew up row ends of head, bring seam and marker together and oversew across cast-on stitches. Stuff head, sew up body leaving a gap, stuff body and sew up gap.

## Forelegs and hind legs

Fold a chenille stem in half for each leg, place fold of chenille stems into wrong side of stitches pulled tight on a thread and sew up side edges of legs enclosing chenille stems inside from tip to wide part. Place another folded chenille stem along wide part and finish sewing up side edges enclosing chenille stems inside. Cut excess chenille stems and sew forelegs to neck and hind legs to body.

## Wings

Fold cast-off stitches in half and oversew. Place wings on thick cardboard and draw round outside edge. Draw a line ¼in (6mm) inside line and cut out. Sandwich cardboard between two pieces of wings and oversew around outside edge enclosing cardboard inside. Pin and sew wings to Bumblebee.

## Antennae

Fold the tip of a chenille stick over and place this fold into wrong side of stitches pulled tight of antenna. Sew up row ends of antenna enclosing chenille stem inside. Cut chenille stem to length of antenna and repeat for the other antenna. Sew antennae to head and bend, as in picture.

## Eyes

Sew a running stitch around outside edge of each eye, pull tight into a ball and secure. Sew eyes to head.

# Hedgehog
# with Hoglets

# Information you'll need

## Materials
Any DK (US: light worsted) yarn
(amounts given are approximate)
**Yarn A** black (5g)
**Yarn B** beige (100g)
**Yarn C** brown (50g)
Oddment of black for embroidery
1 pair of 3.25mm (UK10:US3) needles
Knitters' pins and a blunt-ended needle
for sewing up
Acrylic toy stuffing

## Finished size
Hedgehog measures 9in (23cm) long
Hoglets measure 3¼in (8cm) long

## Tension
26 sts x 34 rows measure 4in (10cm) square
over st-st using 3.25mm needles and DK yarn
before stuffing, or needles to give correct tension.

## Abbreviations
See page 164

## How to make Hedgehog

### Head and body

Beg at nose using the long tail method and yarn A, cast on 12 sts.

**Rows 1 to 4:** Beg with a p row, work 4 rows in rev st-st.

**Rows 5 and 6:** Change to yarn B and k 1 row then p 1 row.

**Row 7:** (K1, m1) twice, k3, m1, k2, m1, k3, (m1, k1) twice (18 sts).

**Row 8 and foll 2 alt rows:** Purl.

**Row 9:** (K1, m1) twice, k6, m1, k2, m1, k6, (m1, k1) twice (24 sts).

**Row 11:** (K1, m1) twice, k9, m1, k2, m1, k9, (m1, k1) twice (30 sts).

**Row 13:** (K1, m1) twice, k12, m1, k2, m1, k12, (m1, k1) twice (36 sts).

**Rows 14 to 16:** Work 3 rows in st-st.

**Row 17:** (K1, m1) twice, k15, m1, k2, m1, k15, (m1, k1) twice (42 sts).

**Rows 18 to 20:** Work 3 rows in st-st.

**Row 21:** (K1, m1) twice, k18, m1, k2, m1, k18, (m1, k1) twice (48 sts).

**Rows 22 to 24:** Work 3 rows in st-st.

**Row 25:** (K1, m1) twice, k21, m1, k2, m1, k21, (m1, k1) twice (54 sts).

**Rows 26 to 28:** Work 3 rows in st-st.

**Row 29:** (K1, m1) twice, k24, m1, k2, m1, k24, (m1, k1) twice (60 sts).

**Rows 30 to 34:** Work 5 rows in st-st. Join on yarn C and work with yarn B and yarn C together, treating them as one strand.

**Row 35:** Knit.

**Row 36:** K12, *place index finger of LH behind LH needle and wind yarn round finger and needle clockwise once, then wind just round needle in the same direction once. Knit st pulling 2 loops through, place these loops on LH needle and k into the back of them. Pull on loops just made to secure (this will be referred to as loop-st); rep from * 35

times more, k12.

**Row 37:** Knit.

**Row 38:** K12, (loop-st) 36 times, k12.

**Rows 39 to 66:** Rep rows 37 and 38, 14 times more.

**Row 67:** K7, (k2tog, k2) to last 5 sts, k5 (48 sts).

**Row 68:** K10 (loop-st) 28 times, k10.

**Row 69:** Knit.

**Row 70:** As row 68.

**Row 71:** K5, (k2tog, k2) to last 3 sts, k3 (38 sts).

**Row 72:** K9 (loop-st) 20 times, k9.

**Row 73:** K4, (k2tog, k2) to last 2 sts, k2 (30 sts).

**Row 74:** K7, (loop-st) 16 times, k7.

**Row 75:** K4, (k2tog, k2) to last 2 sts, k2 (24 sts).

**Row 76:** K6, (loop-st) 12 times, k6.

**Row 77:** K1, k2tog, (k2, k2tog) to last st, k1 (18 sts).

**Row 78:** K4, (loop-st) 10 times, k4.

**Row 79:** K2, (k2tog, k1) to last st, k1 (13 sts).

**Row 80:** K3, (loop-st) 7 times, k3.

**Row 81:** K1, (k2tog, k1) to end (9 sts).

**Row 82:** K2, (loop-st) 5 times, k2.

Break yarn and thread through sts on needle, pull tight and secure by threading yarn a second time through sts.

## Making up Hedgehog

**Note:** Sew up all row-end seams on right side using mattress stitch one stitch in from the edge, unless otherwise stated; a one-stitch seam allowance has been allowed for this.

### Hedgehog

Gather round cast-on stitches of nose, pull tight and secure. Sew up side edges of head and oversew row ends of body leaving a gap. Place a ball of stuffing into nose, stuff head then body and sew up gap.

### Features

Using picture as a guide, mark position of eyes with two pins and embroider eyes in black making a chain stitch for each eye, then a second chain stitch on top of first (see page 163 for how to begin and fasten off invisibly for the embroidery).

# How to make Hoglets

## Head and body

Beg at nose using the long tail method and yarn A, cast on 8 sts.

**Rows 1 to 3:** Beg with a p row, work 3 rows in rev st-st.

**Row 4:** Change to yarn B and p 1 row.

**Row 5:** (K1, m1) twice, k4, (m1, k1) twice (12 sts).

**Row 6 and foll alt row:** Purl.

**Row 7:** (K1, m1) twice, k3, m1, k2, m1, k3, (m1, k1) twice (18 sts).

**Row 9:** (K1, m1) twice, k6, m1, k2, m1, k6, (m1, k1) twice (24 sts).

**Rows 10 to 16:** Beg with a p row, work 7 rows in st-st.

Join on yarn C and work with yarn B and yarn C together, treating them as one strand.

**Row 17:** Knit.

**Row 18:** K5, *k next st and place index finger of LH behind LH needle and wind yarn round finger and needle clockwise once, then just round needle in the same direction once, k st pulling 2 loops through. Place these loops on LH needle and k into the back of them. Pull loop just made sharply down to secure (this will be referred to as loop-st); rep from * 13 times more, k5.

**Row 19:** Knit.

**Row 20:** K5, (loop-st) 14 times, k5.

**Rows 21 to 24:** Rep rows 19 and 20, twice more.

**Row 25:** K1, k2tog, (k2, k2tog) to last st, k1 (18 sts).

**Row 26:** K4, (loop-st) 10 times, k4.

**Row 27:** K2, (K2tog, k1) to last st, k1 (13 sts).

**Row 28:** K3, (loop-st) 7 times, k3.

**Row 29:** K1, (k2tog, k1) to end (9 sts).

**Row 30:** K2, (loop-st) 5 times, k2.

Break yarn and thread through sts on needle, pull tight and secure by threading yarn a second time through sts.

# Making up Hoglets

## Hoglets

Make up Hoglets, as for Hedgehog.

# Fire Ant

# Information you'll need

## Materials

Any DK (US: light worsted) yarn
(amounts given are approximate)
**Yarn A** dark red (50g)
**Yarn B** black (5g)
Oddment of black for embroidery
1 pair of 3.25mm (UK10:US3) needles
Knitters' pins and a blunt-ended needle
for sewing up
Tweezers (optional)
Acrylic toy stuffing
14 chenille stems 12in (30.5cm) long

## Finished size

Fire Ant measures
10½in (26.5cm) long

## Tension

26 sts x 34 rows measure 4in (10cm) square
over st-st using 3.25mm needles and DK
yarn before stuffing, or needles to give
correct tension.

## Abbreviations

See page 164

# How to make Fire Ant

## Head

Using the long tail method and yarn A, cast on 9 sts.

**Row 1 and foll 3 alt rows:** Purl.
**Row 2:** K1, (m1, k1) to end (17 sts).
**Row 4:** K1, (m1, k2) to end (25 sts).
**Row 6:** K1, (m1, k3) to end (33 sts).
**Row 8:** K1, (m1, k4) to end (41 sts).
**Rows 9 to 23:** Work 15 rows in st-st.
**Row 24:** K1, (k2tog, k3) to end (33 sts).
**Row 25 and foll 2 alt rows:** Purl.
**Row 26:** K1, (k2tog, k2) to end (25 sts).
**Row 28:** K1, (k2tog, k1) to end (17 sts).
**Row 30:** K1, (k2tog) to end (9 sts).
Break yarn and thread through sts on needle, pull tight and secure by threading yarn a second time through sts.

### Front piece

Using the long tail method and yarn A, cast on 15 sts.

**Rows 1 and 2:** P 1 row then k 1 row.
**Row 3:** (P2tog, p1) to end (10 sts).
**Row 4:** Knit.
**Row 5:** (P2tog) to end (5 sts).
Break yarn and thread through sts on needle, pull tight and secure by threading yarn a second time through sts.

## First body segment

Using the long tail method and yarn A, cast on 32 sts.

**Row 1:** Purl.
**Row 2:** K5, (m1, k2) 4 times, k8, (m1, k2) 4 times, k3 (40 sts).
**Rows 3 to 7:** Work 5 rows in st-st.
**Row 8:** K8, (k2tog) twice, k16, (k2tog) twice, k8 (36 sts).
**Row 9 and foll 5 alt rows:** Purl.
**Row 10:** K7, (k2tog) twice, k14, (k2tog) twice, k7 (32 sts).
**Row 12:** K6, (k2tog) twice, k12, (k2tog) twice, k6 (28 sts).

**Row 14:** K5, (k2tog) twice, k10, (k2tog) twice, k5 (24 sts).
**Row 16:** K4, (k2tog) twice, k8, (k2tog) twice, k4 (20 sts).
**Row 18:** K1, (k2tog) 4 times, k2, (k2tog) 4 times, k1 (12 sts).
**Row 20:** (K2tog) to end (6 sts).
Break yarn and thread through sts on needle, pull tight and secure by threading yarn a second time through sts.

## Second body segment

Using the long tail method and yarn A, cast on 10 sts.

**Row 1 and foll 2 alt rows:** Purl.
**Row 2:** K1, (m1, k1) to end (19 sts).
**Row 4:** K1, (m1, k2) to end (28 sts).
**Row 6:** K1, (m1, k3) to end (37 sts).
**Rows 7 to 17:** Work 11 rows in st-st.
**Row 18:** K1, (k2tog, k2) to end (28 sts).
**Row 19 and foll alt row:** Purl.
**Row 20:** K1, (k2tog, k1) to end (19 sts).
**Row 22:** K1, (k2tog) to end (10 sts).
Break yarn and thread through sts on needle, pull tight and secure by threading yarn a second time through sts.

## Third and fourth body segments (make 2 pieces)

Using the long tail method and yarn A, cast on 10 sts.

**Row 1 and foll alt row:** Purl.
**Row 2:** K1, (m1, k1) to end (19 sts).
**Row 4:** K1, (m1, k2) to end (28 sts).
**Rows 5 to 13:** Work 9 rows in st-st.
**Row 14:** K1, (k2tog, k1) to end (19 sts).
**Row 15:** Purl.
**Row 16:** K1, (k2tog) to end (10 sts).
Break yarn and thread through sts on needle, pull tight and secure by threading yarn a second time through sts.

## Tail

Using the long tail method and yarn B, cast on 10 sts.

**Row 1 and foll alt row:** Purl.
**Row 2:** K1, (m1, k1) to end (19 sts).
**Row 4:** K1, (m1, k2) to end (28 sts).
**Rows 5 to 21:** Work 17 rows in st-st.
**Row 22:** K1, (k2tog, k1) to end (19 sts).
**Row 23:** Purl.
**Row 24:** K1, (k2tog) to end (10 sts).
Break yarn and thread through sts on needle, pull tight and secure by threading yarn a second time through sts.

## Legs (make 6)

Using the long tail method and yarn A, cast on 10 sts.

**Rows 1 to 19:** Beg with a p row, work 19 rows in st-st.
**Row 20:** K2, k2tog, k2, k2tog, k2 (8 sts).
**Rows 21 to 45:** Work 25 rows in st-st.
Break yarn and thread through sts on needle, pull tight and secure by threading yarn a second time through sts.

## Mandibles (make 2)

Using the long tail method and yarn A, cast on 12 sts.

**Rows 1 to 3:** Beg with a p row, work 3 rows in st-st.
**Row 4:** (K2tog, k1) to end (8 sts).
**Row 5:** Purl.
**Row 6:** (K2tog) to end (4 sts).
Break yarn and thread through sts on needle, pull tight and secure by threading yarn a second time through sts.

## Antennae (make 2)

Using the long tail method and yarn A, cast on 6 sts.

**Rows 1 to 31:** Beg with a p row, work 31 rows in st-st.

Break yarn and thread through sts on needle, pull tight and secure by threading yarn a second time through sts.

# Making up Fire Ant

**Note:** Sew up all row-end seams on right side using mattress stitch one stitch in from the edge, unless otherwise stated; a one-stitch seam allowance has been allowed for this.

## Head and front piece

Gather round cast-on stitches of head, pull tight and secure. Sew up row ends of head leaving a gap, stuff and sew up gap. Sew up row ends of front piece, stuff with tweezers or tip of scissors and pin and sew to front of head.

## First body segment

Sew up side edges of body segment and with this seam underneath, sew across cast-on stitches. Sew this edge to base of head.

## Second body segment

Gather round cast-on stitches, pull tight and secure. Sew up side edges leaving a gap, stuff and sew up gap. Press flat and sew to first body segment.

## Third and fourth body segments

Gather round cast-on stitches, pull tight and secure. Sew up side edges leaving a gap, stuff and sew up gap. Press flat and keep in place by sewing back and forth through centre from one side to the other a few times. Pin and sew segments on top of each other and to top of second body segment.

## Tail

Gather round cast-on stitches, pull tight and secure. Sew up side edges leaving a gap, stuff and sew up gap. Sew tail to underneath of last body segment.

## Legs

Take a chenille stem and fold tip over, place fold into stitches pulled tight on a thread. Sew up side edges of narrowest part of leg enclosing chenille stem inside. Fold another chenille stem in half and place fold at beginning of wider section and sew up side edges around chenille stems. Cut chenille stems to length of leg and repeat for all six legs. Sew legs to sides of second body section and using picture as a guide, bend legs.

## Mandibles

Sew up side edges of mandibles and stuff with tweezers or tip of scissors. Pin and sew cast-on stitches of mandibles to front of head.

## Features

Using picture as a guide, mark position of eyes with two pins and embroider eyes in black making a chain stitch ring for each eye, and fill in ring with chain stitches (see page 163 for how to begin and fasten off invisibly for the embroidery).

## Antennae

Place a chenille stem into stitches pulled tight on a thread of each antennae. Sew up side edges for 1in (2.5cm) enclosing chenille stem inside. Fold tip of antennae over and sew in place. Continue sewing side edges and cut chenille stem to length of antennae. Sew antennae to face and bend.

# Octopus

# Information you'll need

## Materials
Any DK (US: light worsted) yarn
(amounts given are approximate)
**Yarn A** sea green (50g)
**Yarn B** cream (30g)
Oddment of black for embroidery
1 pair of 3.25mm (UK10:US3) needles
Knitters' pins and a blunt-ended needle for sewing up
Acrylic toy stuffing

## Finished size
Octopus measures 17in (43cm) long

## Tension
26 sts x 34 rows measure 4in (10cm) square over st-st using
3.25mm needles and DK yarn before stuffing, or needles to
give correct tension.

## Abbreviations
See page 164

## Special abbreviation
**w1** – wrap 1 stitch: take yarn between
needles to opposite side, slip one
stitch pwise from LH needle to
RH needle and take yarn back
between the needles to first side.

# How to make Octopus

## Body and head

Using the long tail method and yarn A, cast on 7 sts.

**Row 1 and foll 5 alt rows:** Purl.
**Row 2:** (Kfb) to end (14 sts).
**Row 4:** As row 2 (28 sts).
**Row 6:** (Kfb, k3) to end (35 sts).
**Row 8:** (Kfb, k4) to end (42 sts).
**Row 10:** (Kfb, k5) to end (49 sts).
**Row 12:** (Kfb, k6) to end (56 sts).

**Rows 13 to 29:** Work 17 rows in st-st.
**Row 30:** (K2tog, k6) to end (49 sts).
**Rows 31 to 33:** Work 3 rows in st-st.
**Rows 34:** (K2tog, k5) to end (42 sts).
**Rows 35 to 40:** Work 6 rows in st-st, ending on a k row.
**Row 41:** K 1 row to mark row for attaching legs.
**Rows 42 and 43:** K 1 row then p 1 row.
**Row 44:** (K2tog, k4) to end (35 sts).
**Rows 45 and foll 3 alt rows:** Purl.
**Row 46:** (K2tog, k3) to end (28 sts).
**Row 48:** (K2tog, k2) to end (21 sts).
**Row 50:** (K2tog, k1) to end (14 sts).
**Row 52:** (K2tog) to end (7 sts).
Break yarn and thread through sts on needle, pull tight and secure by threading yarn a second time through sts.

## Legs (make 8)

Using the long tail method and yarn A, cast on 80 sts.
**Row 1:** P68, w1 (see special abbreviation), turn.
**Row 2:** S1k, k to end.
**Row 3:** P77, w1, turn.
**Row 4:** S1k, k to end.
**Row 5:** P50, w1, turn.
**Row 6:** S1k, k to end.
**Row 7:** P across all sts.
**Row 8:** Change to yarn B and k 1 row.
**Row 9:** (K1, p1) to end (this row sets moss-st).
**Row 10:** (P1, k1) to end.
**Row 11:** Moss-st 76, w1, turn.
**Row 12:** S1k, moss-st to end.
**Row 13:** Moss-st over all sts.
Cast off loosely kwise.

# Making up Octopus

**Note:** Sew up all row-end seams on right side using mattress stitch one stitch in from the edge, unless otherwise stated; a one-stitch seam allowance has been allowed for this.

## Body and head

Gather round cast-on stitches of head, pull tight and secure. Sew up side edges of body and head leaving a gap, stuff and sew up gap.

## Legs

Fold legs lengthways and sew up side edge. Sew tops of legs side by side to make a ring and place around body around garter stitch row. Sew legs to body above and below garter stitch row.

## Features

Using picture as a guide, mark position of eyes with two pins and embroider eyes in black making a vertical chain stitch for each eye, then a second chain stitch on top of first (see page 163 for how to begin and fasten off invisibly for the embroidery).

# Owl with Owlets

# Information you'll need

## Materials
Any DK (US: light worsted) yarn
(amounts given are approximate)
**Yarn A** cream (80g)
**Yarn B** pale grey (25g)
**Yarn C** dark brown (5g)
**Yarn D** brown (25g)
Oddment of black for embroidery
1 pair of 3.25mm (UK10:US3) needles and
a spare needle of same size
Knitters' pins and a blunt-ended needle for sewing up
Tweezers (optional)
6 chenille stems
Acrylic toy stuffing

## Finished size
Owl measures 8¾in (22cm) high
Owlets measure 5½–6¾in (14–17cm) high

## Tension
26 sts x 34 rows measure 4in (10cm) square over st-st
using 3.25mm needles and DK yarn before stuffing, or
needles to give correct tension.

## Abbreviations
See page 164

# How to make Owl

## Body, head and ears
Using the long tail method and yarn A, cast on 32 sts.
**Row 1 and foll 5 alt rows:** Purl.
**Row 2:** *(K2, m1) twice, k8, (m1, k2) twice; rep from * once (40 sts).
**Row 4:** *(K2, m1) twice, k12, (m1, k2) twice; rep from * once (48 sts).
**Row 6:** *(K2, m1) twice, k16, (m1, k2) twice; rep from * once (56 sts).
**Row 8:** *(K2, m1) twice, k20, (m1, k2) twice; rep from * once (64 sts).
**Row 10:** *(K2, m1) twice, k24, (m1, k2) twice; rep from * once (72 sts).
**Row 12:** *(K2, m1) twice, k28, (m1, k2) twice; rep from * once (80 sts).
**Rows 13 to 19:** Work 7 rows in st-st.
**Row 20:** K2tog, k to last 2 sts, k2tog (78 sts).
**Row 21:** P2tog, p to last 2 sts, p2tog (76 sts).
**Rows 22 to 29:** Rep rows 20 and 21, 4 times more (60 sts).
**Rows 30 to 51:** Work 22 rows in st-st.
**Row 52:** (K2tog, k3) to end (48 sts).
**Row 53 and foll alt row:** Purl.
**Row 54:** (K2tog, k2) to end (36 sts).
**Row 56:** K2, (m1, k2) to end (53 sts).
**Rows 57 to 77:** Work 21 rows in st-st.
**Row 78:** K12, (m1, k1) 4 times, k22, (m1, k1) 4 times, k11 (61 sts).
**Row 79 and foll 2 alt rows:** Purl.
**Row 80:** K14, (m1, k1) 4 times, k26, (m1, k1) 4 times, k13 (69 sts).
**Row 82:** K16, (m1, k1) 4 times, k30, (m1, k1) 4 times, k15 (77 sts).
**Row 84:** K18, (m1, k1) 4 times, k34, (m1, k1) 4 times, k17 (85 sts).
**Row 85:** Purl.
Cast off.

## Eyes (make 2)
Using the long tail method and yarn B, cast on 45 sts and beg in rev st-st.
**Rows 1 to 3:** Beg with a p row, work 3 rows in rev st-st.
**Row 4:** Change to yarn A and p 1 row.
**Row 5:** (K2tog, k3) to end (36 sts).
**Row 6 and foll 2 alt rows:** Purl.
**Row 7:** (K2tog, k2) to end (27 sts).
**Row 9:** (K2tog, k1) to end (18 sts).
**Row 11:** (K2tog) to end (9 sts).
Break yarn and thread through sts on needle, pull tight and secure by threading yarn a second time through sts.

## Beak
Using the long tail method and yarn C, cast on 16 sts.
**Rows 1 to 5:** Beg with a p row, work 5 rows in st-st.
**Row 6:** K1, (k2tog, k1) to end (11 sts).
**Row 7:** Purl.
**Row 8:** K2tog, (k1, k2tog) to end (7 sts).
Break yarn and thread through sts on needle, pull tight and secure by threading yarn a second time through sts.

## Talons (make 2)
Using the long tail method and yarn A, cast on 10 sts.

### First toe
**Rows 1 to 3:** Beg with a p row, work 3 rows in st-st. Break yarn and set aside.
### Second toe
**Rows 1 to 3:** Rep instructions as for first toe but do not break yarn.
### Join toes
**Row 4:** K across sts of second toe and then with same yarn cont knitting across sts of first toe (20 sts).
**Rows 5 to 9:** Work 5 rows in st-st.
**Row 10:** K2tog, (k1, k2tog) to end (13 sts).
**Row 11:** Purl.
**Row 12:** K1, (k2tog, k1) to end (9 sts).
Break yarn and thread through sts on needle, pull tight and secure by threading yarn a second time through sts.

## Tail
Using the long tail method and yarn A, cast on 100 sts.
**Row 1:** P4, (s1p, p6) to last 5 sts, s1p, p4.
**Row 2:** K4, (s1p, k6) to last 5 sts, s1p, k4.
**Row 3:** K2tog, (k5, k2tog) to end (85 sts).
**Row 4:** Purl.
Join on yarn D and work in yarn A and D, carrying yarn loosely up side of work, and shape:
**Row 5:** Yarn D-k2tog, (k1, m1, k1, m1, k1, k3tog) to last 5 sts, k1, m1, k1, m1, k1, k2tog.
**Row 6:** Knit.
**Rows 7 and 8:** Yarn-A, k 1 row then p 1 row.
**Rows 9 and 10:** Yarn D-rep rows 5 and 6 once.
**Row 11:** Yarn A-knit.
**Row 12:** P2tog, (p3, p3tog) to last 5 sts, p3, p2tog (57 sts).
**Rows 13 to 16:** Beg with a k row, work 4 rows in st-st.
**Rows 17 and 18:** Yarn D-work 2 rows in g-st.
**Rows 19 and 20:** Cont in yarn A-k 1 row

then p 1 row.

**Row 21:** K12, k2tog tbl, k2tog, k25, k2tog tbl, k2tog, k12 (53 sts).

**Rows 22 to 24:** P 1 row then k 2 rows.

**Row 25:** K11, k2tog tbl, k2tog, k23, k2tog tbl, k2tog, k11 (49 sts).

**Rows 26 to 28:** P 1 row then k 2 rows.

**Row 29:** K10, k2tog tbl, k2tog, k21, k2tog tbl, k2tog, k10 (45 sts).

**Rows 30 to 32:** P 1 row then k 2 rows.

**Row 33:** K9, k2tog tbl, k2tog, k19, k2tog tbl, k2tog, k9 (41 sts).

Cast off kwise.

## Wings

Using the long tail method and yarn A, cast on 76 sts.

**Row 1 and foll 4 alt rows:** Purl.

**Row 2:** *K14, (m1, k2) 6 times, k12; rep from * once (88 sts).

**Row 4:** *K19, (m1, k2) 4 times, k17; rep from * once (96 sts).

**Row 6:** *K21, (m1, k2) 4 times, k19; rep from * once (104 sts).

**Row 8:** *K23, (m1, k2) 4 times, k21; rep from * once (112 sts).

**Row 10:** *K25, (m1, k2) 4 times, k23; rep from * once (120 sts).

**Rows 11 and 12:** P 1 row then k 1 row.

**Rows 13 to 21:** Change to yarn D and beg with a p row, work 9 rows in st-st.

**Row 22:** Change to yarn B and k60, turn and work on these 60 sts.

**\*\*Row 23:** Purl.

**Row 24:** (K2tog) twice, k23, k2tog tbl, k2, k2tog, k23, k2tog, k2tog tbl (54 sts).

**Row 25 and foll 7 alt rows:** Purl.

**Row 26:** (K2tog) twice, k20, k2tog tbl, k2, k2tog, k20, k2tog, k2tog tbl (48 sts).

**Row 28:** (K2tog) twice, k17, k2tog tbl, k2, k2tog, k17, k2tog, k2tog tbl (42 sts).

**Row 30:** (K2tog) twice, k14, k2tog tbl, k2, k2tog, k14, k2tog, k2tog tbl (36 sts).

**Row 32:** (K2tog) twice, k11, k2tog tbl, k2, k2tog, k11, k2tog, k2tog tbl (30 sts).

**Row 34:** (K2tog) twice, k8, k2tog tbl, k2, k2tog, k8, k2tog, k2tog tbl (24 sts).

**Row 36:** (K2tog) twice, k5, k2tog tbl, k2, k2tog, k5, k2tog, k2tog tbl (18 sts).

**Row 38:** (K2tog) twice, k2, k2tog tbl, k2, k2tog, k2, k2tog, k2tog tbl (12 sts).

**Row 40:** (K2tog) to end (6 sts).

**Row 41:** Purl.

Break yarn and thread yarn through sts on needle, pull tight and secure by threading yarn a second time through sts.

### Second wing

**Row 42:** Rejoin yarn B to rem sts and k 1 row (60 sts).

**Rows 43 to 61:** Complete second wing from ** to end, as for first wing.

## Making up Owl

**Note:** Sew up all row-end seams on right side using mattress stitch one stitch in from the edge, unless otherwise stated; a one-stitch seam allowance has been allowed for this.

### Body, head and ears

Fold cast-on stitches in half and oversew. Sew up row ends of head, and with seam at centre back, sew across top of head. Sew up side edges leaving a gap, stuff, pushing stuffing into tail and small balls of stuffing into ears and sew up gap.

### Eyes and features

Sew up side edges of eyes and pin and sew eyes to head. Using picture as a guide, embroider pupil in black and make a chain stitch ring at the centre of each eye and fill in the centre with chain stitches (see page 163 for how to begin and fasten off the embroidery invisibly).

### Beak

Sew up side edges of beak and stuff beak with tweezers or tip of scissors. With seam at centre back, sew across cast-on stitches. Sew beak to head.

### Talons

Sew up toes of talons, stuff and sew up side edges. Embroider a claw in black down front of each toe using straight stitches. Place Owl on a flat surface, position talons and sew in place.

### Tail

Sew up side edges of tail and with this seam at centre of inside edge, sew across lower edge. Pin and sew tail to Owl.

### Wings

Fold each wing bringing side edges together and oversew side edges and around points. Place wings on back of Owl and sew in place.

# How to make Owlets

## Small Owlet
### Body, head and ears

Using the long tail method and yarn A cast on 20 sts and work in g-st.

**Row 1:** *(Kfb) twice, k6, (kfb) twice; rep from * once (28 sts).

**Row 2 and foll alt row:** Knit.

**Row 3:** *(K1, kfb) twice, k6, (kfb, k1) twice; rep from * once (36 sts).

**Row 5:** *(K2, kfb) twice, k6, (kfb, k2) twice; rep from * once (44 sts).

**Rows 6 to 10:** Work 5 rows in g-st.

**Row 11:** K2tog, k to last 2 sts, k2tog (42 sts).

**Rows 12 to 16:** Rep row 11, 5 times more (32 sts). **

**Rows 17 and 18:** Work 2 rows in g-st.

**Rows 19 to 24:** Change to yarn D and work 6 rows in g-st.

***Row 25:** (K2tog, k2) to end (24 sts).

**Rows 26 to 30:** Work 5 rows in g-st.

**Row 31:** K5, (kfb) 3 times, k8, (kfb) 3 times, k5 (30 sts).

**Rows 32 to 46:** Work 15 rows in g-st.

**Row 47:** K6, (m1, k1) 4 times, k11, (m1, k1) 4 times, k5 (38 sts).

**Row 48:** Knit.

**Row 49:** K8, (m1, k1) 4 times, k15, (m1, k1) 4 times, k7 (46 sts).

**Rows 50 and 51:** K 2 rows.
Cast off in g-st.

## Medium Owlet
### Body, head and ears

**Rows 1 to 16:** Using yarn D, work as for small Owlet from beg to **.

**Rows 17 to 26:** Cont in yarn D and work 10 rows in g-st.

**Rows 27 to 30:** Change to yarn B and work 4 rows in g-st.

**Rows 31 to 57:** Cont in yarn B and work as for small Owlet from *** to end.

## Large Owlet
### Body, head and ears

**Rows 1 to 16:** Using yarn B, work as for small Owlet from beg to **.

**Rows 17 to 36:** Change to yarn D and work 20 rows in g-st.

**Rows 37 and 38:** Change to yarn A and work 2 rows in g-st.

**Rows 39 to 65:** Cont in yarn A and work as for small Owlet from *** to end.

## Eyes (make 2 per Owlet)

Using the long tail method and yarn A, cast on 30 sts.

**Rows 1 and 2:** P 2 rows.

**Row 3:** (K2tog, k1) to end (20 sts).

**Row 4:** Purl.

**Row 5:** (K2tog) to end (10 sts).
Break yarn and thread through sts on needle, pull tight and secure by threading yarn a second time through sts.

## Beak (make 1 for each Owlet)

Using the long tail method and yarn C, cast on 10 sts.

**Rows 1 to 3:** Beg with a p row, work 3 rows in st-st.

**Row 4:** K1, (k2tog, k1) to end (7 sts).
Break yarn and thread through sts on needle, pull tight and secure by threading yarn a second time through sts.

## Wings (make 2 per Owlet, using yarn D for small Owlet; yarn B for medium Owlet; yarn A for large Owlet)

Using the long tail method and yarn required, cast on 12 sts.

**Row 1:** Purl.

**Row 2:** *K1, (m1, k1) 5 times; rep from * once (22 sts).

**Rows 3 to 5:** Beg with a p row, work 3 rows in st-st.

**Row 6:** (K2tog, k7, k2tog tbl) twice (18 sts).

**Row 7 and foll 3 alt rows:** Purl.

**Row 8:** (K2tog, k5, k2tog tbl) twice (14 sts).

**Row 10:** (K2tog, k3, k2tog tbl) twice (10 sts).

**Row 12:** (K2tog, k1, k2tog tbl) twice (6 sts).

**Row 14:** (K2tog) to end (3 sts).
Break yarn and thread through sts on needle, pull tight and secure by threading yarn a second time through sts.

## Talons (make 2 per Owlet)

Using the long tail method and yarn A, cast on 8 sts.
Beg with a p row, work 13 rows in st-st.
Break yarn and thread through sts on needle, pull tight and secure by threading yarn a second time through sts.

## Making up Owlets

**Note:** Sew up all row-end seams on right side using mattress stitch one stitch in from the edge, unless otherwise stated; a one-stitch seam allowance has been allowed for this.

### Body, head and ears

Fold cast-on stitches in half and oversew. Oversew row ends of head and with seam at centre back, sew across top of head. Stuff head, oversew row ends of body leaving a gap, stuff Owlet pushing a small ball of stuffing into ears and tail and sew up gap.

### Eyes

Sew up side edges of each eye and oversew eyes together at centre. Pin and sew eyes to head.

### Beak

Sew up side edges of beak and stuff beak with tweezers or tip of scissors. With seam at centre back, sew across cast-on stitches. Sew beak to head.

### Features

Using picture as a guide, embroider eyes in black. For open eyes make a vertical chain stitch for each eye, then a second chain stitch on top of first. For sleeping eyes make a straight horizontal stitch (see page 163 for how to begin and fasten off invisibly for the embroidery).

### Wings

Fold wings in half and sew back and forth around open edge. Sew wings to Owlets.

### Talons

For each talon, cut a bundle of 3 chenille stems 1½in (4cm) long and place inside talons, gather round cast-on stitches, pull tight and secure. Sew up side edges of talons enclosing chenille stems inside. Bend talons into a U-shape and embroider a claw in black down front of each toe using straight stitches. Sew talons to Owlets.

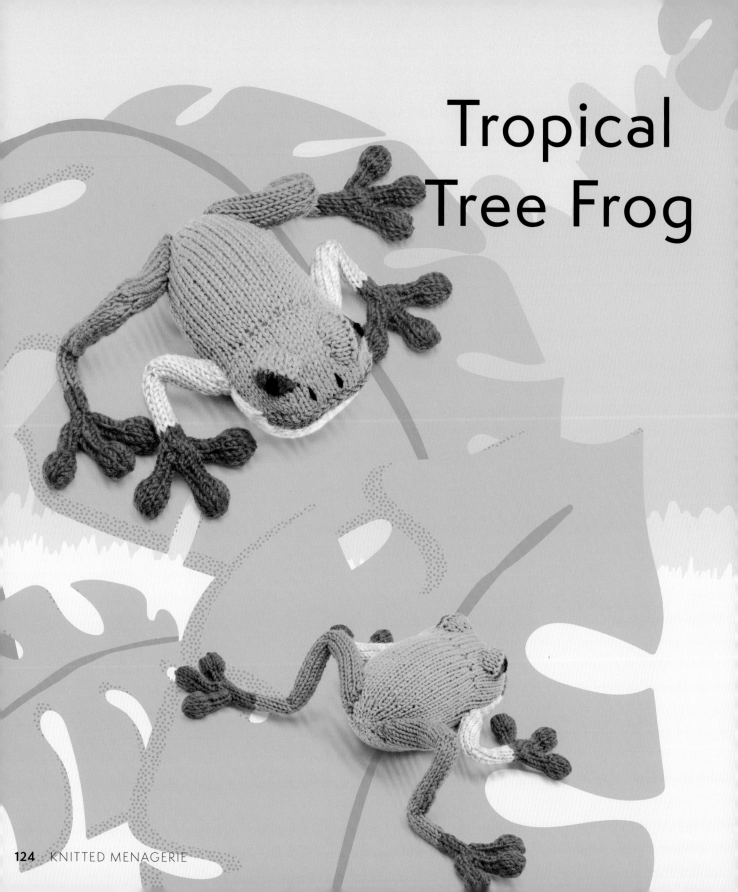

# Tropical Tree Frog

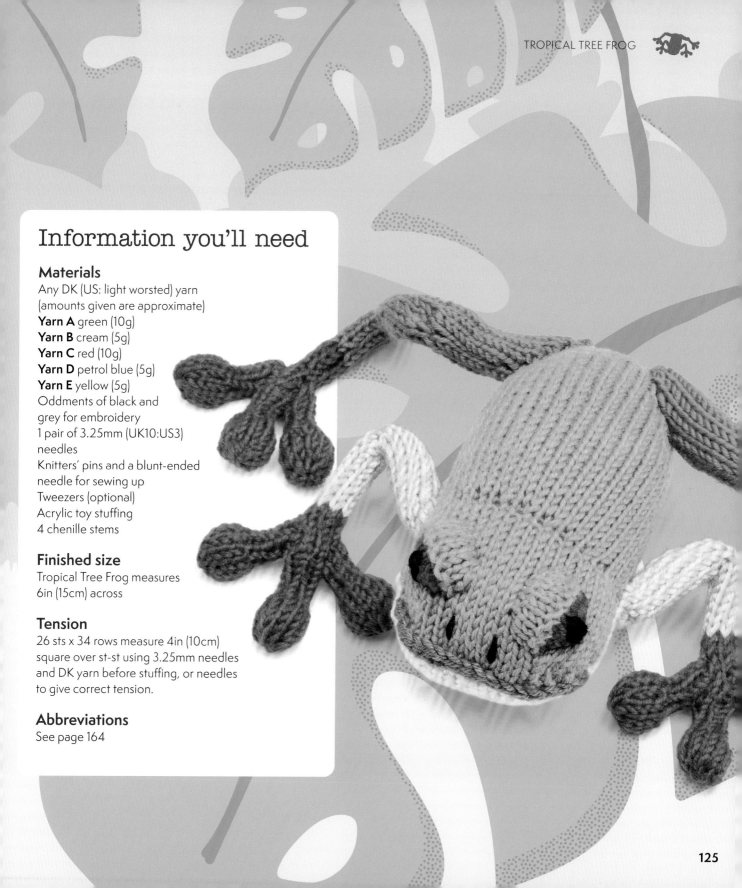

# Information you'll need

## Materials

Any DK (US: light worsted) yarn
(amounts given are approximate)
**Yarn A** green (10g)
**Yarn B** cream (5g)
**Yarn C** red (10g)
**Yarn D** petrol blue (5g)
**Yarn E** yellow (5g)
Oddments of black and
grey for embroidery
1 pair of 3.25mm (UK10:US3)
needles
Knitters' pins and a blunt-ended
needle for sewing up
Tweezers (optional)
Acrylic toy stuffing
4 chenille stems

## Finished size

Tropical Tree Frog measures
6in (15cm) across

## Tension

26 sts x 34 rows measure 4in (10cm)
square over st-st using 3.25mm needles
and DK yarn before stuffing, or needles
to give correct tension.

## Abbreviations

See page 164

# How to make Tropical Tree Frog

## Underside of body
Using the long tail method and yarn A, cast on 6 sts.

**Row 1:** Purl.
**Row 2:** (K1, m1, k1, m1, k1) twice (10 sts).
**Rows 3 to 5:** Work 3 rows in st-st.
**Row 6:** K1, m1, k3, m1, k2, m1, k3, m1, k1 (14 sts).
**Rows 7 to 9:** Work 3 rows in st-st.
**Row 10:** K1, m1, k3, m1, k6, m1, k3, m1, k1 (18 sts).
**Rows 11 to 13:** Work 3 rows in st-st.
**Row 14:** K1, m1, k3, m1, k10, m1, k3, m1, k1 (22 sts).
**Rows 15 to 31:** Work 17 rows in st-st.
**Row 32:** K4, (k2tog) 7 times, k4 (15 sts).
**Row 33:** Purl.
Change to yarn B and shape:
**Row 34:** K3, (m1, k1) 10 times, k2 (25 sts).
**Rows 35 to 41:** Work 7 rows in st-st.

**Row 42:** K2tog, k to last 2 sts, k2tog (23 sts).
**Row 43:** Purl.
**Rows 44 and 45:** Rep rows 42 and 43 once (21 sts).
**Row 46:** K2tog, k2, k2tog, k9, k2tog, k2, k2tog (17 sts).
**Row 47:** P2tog, p to last 2 sts, p2tog (15 sts).
**Row 48:** K2tog, k to last 2 sts, k2tog (13 sts).
**Row 49:** P2tog, p to last 2 sts, p2tog (11 sts).
Cast off.

## Top of body
Using yarn A throughout, work as for underside of body.

## Hind legs (make 2)
Using the long tail method and yarn C, cast on 9 sts.

**Rows 1 to 7:** Beg with a p row, work 7 rows in st-st.
**Rows 8 to 15:** Change to yarn D and work 8 rows in st-st.
**Row 16:** (K2tog, k1) to end (6 sts).
**Row 17:** Purl.
**Row 18:** K1, (m1, k1) to end (11 sts).
**Rows 19 to 33:** Work 15 rows in st-st.
**Row 34:** K2tog, (k1, k2tog) to end (7 sts).
**Row 35:** Purl.
**Row 36:** K1, (m1, k1) to end (13 sts).
**Rows 37 to 45:** Work 9 rows in st-st.
**Row 46:** K2tog, k to last 2 sts, k2tog (11 sts).
**Row 47:** Purl.

**Rows 48 to 53:** Rep rows 46 and 47, 3 times more (5 sts).
**Row 54:** K2tog, k1, k2tog (3 sts).
Break yarn and thread through sts on needle, pull tight and secure by threading yarn a second time through sts.

## Forearms (make 2)
Using the long tail method and yarn C, cast on 9 sts.

**Rows 1 to 5:** Beg with a p row, work 5 rows in st-st.
**Rows 6 to 13:** Change to yarn E and work 8 rows in st-st.
**Row 14:** (K2tog, k1) to end (6 sts).
**Row 15:** Purl.
**Row 16:** K1, (m1, k1) to end (11 sts).
**Rows 17 to 25:** Work 9 rows in st-st.
**Row 26:** K2tog, k to last 2 sts, k2tog (9 sts).
**Row 27:** P2tog, p to last 2 sts, p2tog (7 sts).
**Row 28:** As row 26 (5 sts).
**Row 29:** P2tog, p1, p2tog (3 sts).
Break yarn and thread through sts on needle, pull tight and secure by threading yarn a second time through sts.

## Toes (make 12)
Using the long tail method and yarn C, cast on 7 sts.

**Rows 1 to 7:** Beg with a p row, work 7 rows in st-st.
**Row 8:** K1, (m1, k1) to end (13 sts).
**Rows 9 to 11:** Work 3 rows in st-st.
**Row 12:** K1, (k2tog, k1) to end (9 sts).
Break yarn and thread through sts on needle, pull tight and secure by threading yarn a second time through sts.

## Eyes (make 2)
Using the long tail method and yarn A, cast on 5 sts.

**Row 1 and foll alt row:** Purl.
**Row 2:** K1, (m1, k1) to end (9 sts).
**Rows 4 and 5:** Work 2 rows in g-st.

**Rows 6 to 8:** Change to yarn C and beg with a k row, work 3 rows in st-st. Break yarn and thread through sts on needle, pull tight and second by threading yarn a second time through sts.

## Making up Tropical Tree Frog

**Note:** Sew up all row-end seams on right side using mattress stitch one stitch in from the edge, unless otherwise stated; a one-stitch seam allowance has been allowed for this.

### Body
Place wrong sides of top and underside of body together matching all edges and sew around outside edge leaving a gap, stuff and sew up gap.

## Hind legs
Fold a chenille stem in half and place on wrong side of leg and sew up narrow end of leg enclosing chenille stem inside. Sew up middle of leg enclosing a little stuffing inside with tweezers or tip of scissors. Sew up to decrease stitches and stuff. Cut chenille stem to length of leg, repeat for second leg, sew legs to body and bend legs.

## Forearms
Fold a chenille stem in half, place on wrong side of forearm and sew up narrow end of forearm enclosing chenille stem inside. Sew up straight edges of forearm enclosing a little stuffing inside with tweezers or tip of scissors. Cut chenille stem to length of forearm, repeat for second forearm, sew forearms to body and bend.

## Toes
Sew up ball of toe and stuff with a tiny ball of stuffing pushing stuffing in with tweezers or tip of scissors and sew up side edges. Repeat for 12 toes and sew a toe to ends of hind legs and forearms and sew two toes to each side of the middle toe.

## Eyes
Stuff eyes and pin and sew to head facing outwards.

## Features
Using picture as a guide, embroider eyes in black making a long vertical chain stitch for each eye, then a second chain stitch on top of first. Embroider two nostrils using straight stitches. Embroider mouth in grey making two chain stitch rows close together (see page 163 for how to begin and fasten off invisibly for the embroidery).

# Lovebirds

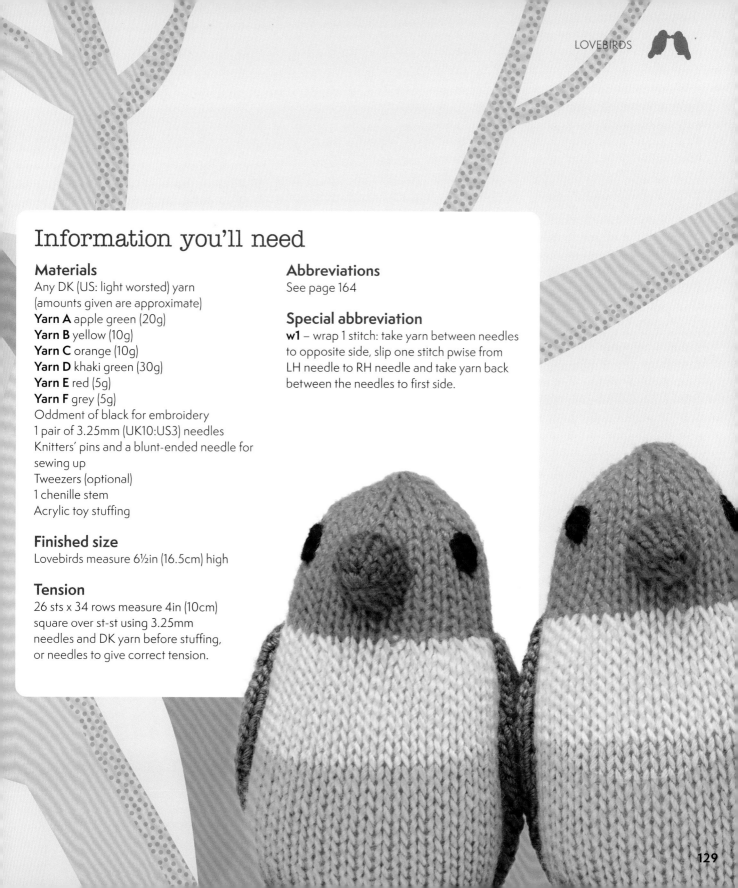

# Information you'll need

## Materials
Any DK (US: light worsted) yarn
(amounts given are approximate)
**Yarn A** apple green (20g)
**Yarn B** yellow (10g)
**Yarn C** orange (10g)
**Yarn D** khaki green (30g)
**Yarn E** red (5g)
**Yarn F** grey (5g)
Oddment of black for embroidery
1 pair of 3.25mm (UK10:US3) needles
Knitters' pins and a blunt-ended needle for
sewing up
Tweezers (optional)
1 chenille stem
Acrylic toy stuffing

## Finished size
Lovebirds measure 6½in (16.5cm) high

## Tension
26 sts x 34 rows measure 4in (10cm)
square over st-st using 3.25mm
needles and DK yarn before stuffing,
or needles to give correct tension.

## Abbreviations
See page 164

## Special abbreviation
**w1** – wrap 1 stitch: take yarn between needles
to opposite side, slip one stitch pwise from
LH needle to RH needle and take yarn back
between the needles to first side.

# How to make Lovebird (make a pair)

## Body and head

Using the long tail method and yarn A, cast on 18 sts and place a marker at centre of cast-on stitches.

**Row 1 and foll 2 alt rows:** Purl.
**Row 2:** K2, (m1, k2) to end (26 sts).
**Row 4:** *(K2, m1) twice, k5, (m1, k2) twice; rep from * once (34 sts).
**Row 6:** *(K2, m1) twice, k9, (m1, k2) twice; rep from * once (42 sts).
**Row 7:** Purl.
**Row 8:** K34, w1 (see special abbreviation), turn.
**Row 9:** S1p, p26, w1, turn.
**Row 10:** S1k, k to end.
**Rows 11 to 13:** Work 3 rows in st-st.
**Rows 14 to 25:** Rep rows 8 to 13 twice more.
**Rows 26 to 28:** Change to yarn B and work rows 8 to 10 once.
**Rows 29 to 35:** Work 7 rows in st-st. Change to yarn C and dec:
**Row 36:** K9, (k2tog) 5 times, k4, (k2tog) 5 times, k9 (32 sts).
**Rows 37 to 47:** Work 11 rows in st-st.
**Row 48:** (K2tog, k2) to end (24 sts).
**Row 49 and foll alt row:** Purl.
**Row 50:** (K2tog, k1) to end (16 sts).
**Row 52:** (K2tog) to end (8 sts).
Break yarn and thread through sts on needle, pull tight and secure by threading yarn a second time through sts.

## Tail

Using the long tail method and yarn D, cast on 20 sts.

**Row 1:** Purl.
**Row 2:** (K4, m1, k2, m1, k4) twice (24 sts).
**Rows 3 to 17:** Beg with a p row, work 15 rows in st-st.
**Row 18:** Cast off 6 sts, k11 (12 sts now on RH needle), cast off rem 6 sts and fasten off (12 sts).
**Rows 19 to 29:** Rejoin yarn to sts and beg with a p row, work 11 rows in st-st. Cast off.

## Wings

Using the long tail method and yarn D, cast on 56 sts.

**Row 1 and foll 3 alt rows:** Purl.
**Row 2:** (K13, m1, k2, m1, k13) twice (60 sts).
**Row 4:** (K14, m1, k2, m1, k14) twice (64 sts).
**Row 6:** (K15, m1, k2, m1, k15) twice (68 sts).
**Row 8:** (K16, m1, k2, m1, k16) twice (72 sts).
**Rows 9 to 13:** Work 5 rows in st-st.
**Row 14:** *K16, k2tog tbl, k2tog, k16; rep from * once (68 sts).
**Row 15 and foll 4 alt rows:** Purl.
**Row 16:** *K2tog, k13, k2tog tbl, k2tog, k13, k2tog tbl; rep from * once (60 sts).
**Row 18:** *K13, k2tog tbl, k2tog, k13; rep from * once (56 sts).

**Row 20:** *K2tog, k10, k2tog tbl, k2tog, k10, k2tog tbl; rep from * once (48 sts).
**Row 22:** *K10, k2tog tbl, k2tog, k10; rep from * once (44 sts).
**\*\*Row 24:** K2tog, k7, k2tog tbl, k2tog, k7, k2tog tbl, turn and work on these 18 sts.
**Row 25 and foll 2 alt rows:** Purl.
**Row 26:** K2tog, k5, k2tog tbl, k2tog, k5, k2tog tbl (14 sts).
**Row 28:** K2tog, k3, k2tog tbl, k2tog, k3, k2tog tbl (10 sts).
**Row 30:** (K2tog) to end (5 sts).
Break yarn and thread through sts on needle, pull tight and secure by threading yarn a second time through sts.
**Rows 31 to 37:** Rejoin yarn to rem sts and work from \*\* to end.

## Beak

Using the long tail method and yarn E, cast on 14 sts.
**Row 1:** P2tog, p8, w1, turn.

**Row 2:** S1k, k6, w1, turn.
**Row 3:** S1p, p to last 2 sts, p2tog (12 sts).
**Row 4:** Knit.
**Row 5:** P2tog, p6, w1, turn.
**Row 6:** S1k, k4, w1, turn.
**Row 7:** S1p, p to last 2 sts, p2tog (10 sts).
**Row 8:** K2tog, k to last 2 sts, k2tog (8 sts).
**Row 9:** P2tog, p3, w1, turn.
**Row 10:** S1k, k2, w1, turn.
**Row 11:** S1p, p to last 2 sts, p2tog (6 sts).
Break yarn and thread through sts on needle, pull tight and secure by threading yarn a second time through sts.

## Centre claw and back claw (make 2)

Using the long tail method and yarn F, cast on 7 sts.
**Rows 1 to 11:** Beg with a p row, work 11 rows in st-st.
Break yarn and thread through sts on needle, pull tight and secure by threading yarn a second time through sts.

## Side claws (make 4)

Using the long tail method and yarn F, cast on 7 sts.
**Rows 1 to 4:** Beg with a p row, work 4 rows in st-st, ending with a k row.
**Row 5:** P2tog, p3, p2tog (5 sts).
**Row 6:** K2tog, k1, k2tog (3 sts).
Break yarn and thread through sts on needle, pull tight and secure by threading yarn a second time through sts.

# Making up Lovebirds

**Note:** Sew up all row-end seams on right side using mattress stitch one stitch in from the edge, unless otherwise stated; a one-stitch seam allowance has been allowed for this.

## Body and head

Sew up side edges of body and head leaving a gap, bring marker and seam together and sew across cast-on stitches. Stuff head then body and sew up gap.

## Tail

Sew up side edges of wide part of tail and with this seam at centre of underneath sew across cast-off stitches. Stuff tail lightly and pin and sew tail to Lovebird sewing edges of patch to lower back.

## Wings

Bring side edges of wings together and oversew and sew round points. With seam at centre of inside edge, sew across cast-on stitches. Sew cast-on stitches to neck of Lovebird and sew around all edges.

## Beak

Sew up side edges of beak and stuff beak with tweezers or tip of scissors. Sew beak to head.

## Features

Using picture as a guide, mark position of eyes with two pins and embroider eyes in black making a ring of chain stitch and fill ring in using chain stitches (see page 163 for how to begin and fasten off invisibly for the embroidery).

## Claws

Cut chenille stem in half. Take each half and fold in half. Place each fold into stitches pulled tight on a thread of centre and back claw. Sew up side edges, cut chenille stems to length of claws and gather round cast-on stitches, pull tight and secure. Sew up straight row ends of side claws and stuff with tweezers or tip of scissors. Sew side claws to centre claws, one each side. Sew claws to underneath of Lovebird.

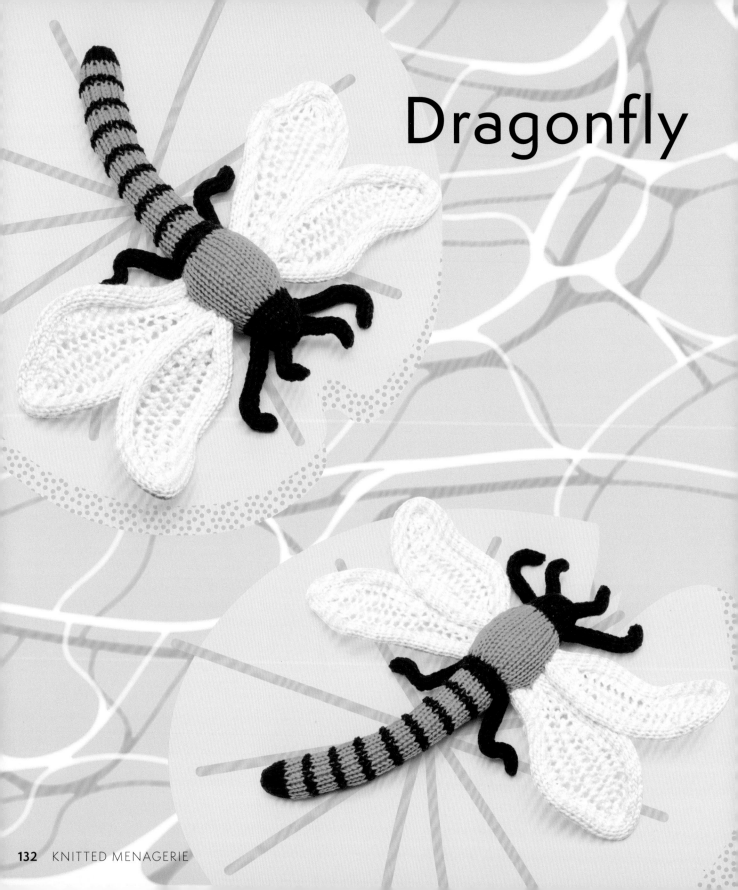

# Dragonfly

# Information you'll need

## Materials
Any DK (US: light worsted) yarn
(amounts given are approximate)
**Yarn A** black (5g)
**Yarn B** azure blue (5g)
**Yarn C** white (10g)
1 pair of 3.25mm (UK12:US2) needles
A blunt-ended needle for sewing up
Acrylic toy stuffing
16 white and 5 black chenille stems

## Finished size
Dragonfly measures 9in (23cm)
across

## Tension
26 sts x 34 rows measure 4in (10cm)
square over st-st using 3.25mm
needles and DK yarn before stuffing,
or needles to give correct tension.

## Abbreviations
See page 164

# How to make Dragonfly

## Body and head

Using the long tail method and yarn A, cast on 10 sts.

**Row 1:** Purl.
**Row 2:** K2, (m1, k2) to end (14 sts).
**Rows 3 to 5:** Beg with a p row, work 3 rows in st-st.
Join on yarn B and work in stripes with yarn A and B, carrying yarn loosely up side of work.
**Rows 6 to 9:** Yarn B-work 4 rows in st-st.
**Rows 10 and 11:** Yarn A-g-st 2 rows.
**Rows 12 to 51:** Rep rows 6 to 11, 6 times more, then rows 6 to 9 once.
**Row 52:** Yarn A-(k2, m1) twice, k6, (m1, k2) twice (18 sts).
**Rows 53 to 55:** Work 3 rows in g-st.
**Row 56:** Yarn B-k 1 row.
**Row 57:** P2, (m1, p2) to end (26 sts).
**Rows 58 to 71:** Beg with a k row, work 14 rows in st-st.
Change to yarn A and shape, as foll:
**Row 72:** K2, (k2tog, k2) to end (20 sts).
**Row 73:** (P1 tbl) to end.
**Rows 74 to 79:** Work 6 rows in st-st.
**Row 80:** (K2tog) to end (10 sts).
**Row 81:** (P2tog) to end (5 sts).
Break yarn and thread through sts on needle, pull tight and secure by threading yarn a second time through sts.

## Wings (make 4 pieces)

Using the long tail method and yarn C, cast on 8 sts.
Beg with a p row, work in st-st for 9in (23cm).
Cast off.

### Upper wing lace (make 2 pieces)

Using the long tail method and yarn C, cast on 2 sts.
**Row 1:** K1, yf, k1 (3 sts).
**Row 2:** K1, (yf, k1) twice (5 sts).
**Row 3:** K2, yf, k1, yf, k2 (7 sts).
**Row 4:** K1, (yf, k2tog) to end.
**Rows 5 to 35:** Rep row 4, 31 times more.
Break yarn and thread through sts on needle, pull tight and secure by threading yarn a second time through sts.

### Lower wing lace (make 2 pieces)

Using the long tail method and yarn C, cast on 4 sts.
**Row 1:** K1, (yf, k1) 3 times (7 sts).
**Row 2:** K1, (yf, k2tog) to end.
**Rows 3 to 13:** Rep row 2, 11 times more.
**Row 14:** K1, yf, k2, (yf, k2tog) twice (8 sts).
**Row 15:** K1, (yf, k2tog) to last st, yf, k1 (9 sts).
**Rows 16 to 27:** Rep row 2, 12 times more.

**Row 28:** K1, (yf, k2tog) 3 times, k2tog (8 sts).
**Row 29:** K2tog, (yf, k2tog) 3 times (7 sts).
**Rows 30 to 35:** Rep row 2, 6 times more.
Break yarn and thread through sts on needle, pull tight and secure by threading yarn a second time through sts.

## Legs (make 4)

Using the long tail method and yarn A, cast on 6 sts.
**Rows 1 to 19:** Beg with a p row, work 19 rows in st-st.
Break yarn and thread through sts on needle, pull tight and secure by threading yarn a second time through sts.

## Antennae (make 2)

Using the long tail method and yarn A, cast on 6 sts.
**Rows 1 to 9:** Beg with a p row, work 9 rows in st-st.
Break yarn and thread through sts on needle, pull tight and secure by threading yarn a second time through sts.

## Making up Dragonfly

**Note:** Sew up all row-end seams on right side using mattress stitch one stitch in from the edge, unless otherwise stated; a one-stitch seam allowance has been allowed for this.

### Body and head

Gather round cast-on stitches, pull tight and secure. Sew up side edges of body, stuffing body as you sew. Sew up upper body and head leaving a gap, stuff and sew up gap.

### Wings

Take four white chenille stems and place wings around chenille stems and sew up side edges enclosing chenille stems inside. Cut chenille stems to length of wings. Using picture as a guide, bend wings round and oversew outside edge of wing lace to underneath of wings. Sew wings to upper body.

### Legs

Place a black chenille stem into stitches pulled tight on a thread on wrong side of each leg and sew up side edges of legs, enclosing chenille stems inside. Cut chenille stems to length of legs. Bend legs as shown in picture and sew to Dragonfly.

### Antennae

Make up as for legs and sew to head at front.

# Lizard

# Information you'll need

## Materials
Any DK (US: light worsted) yarn
(amounts given are approximate)
**Yarn A** pale green (30g)
**Yarn B** buttermilk (5g)
**Yarn C** dark green (20g)
Oddment of black for embroidery
1 pair of 3.25mm (UK10:US3) needles
Yarn bobbin
Knitters' pins and a blunt-ended needle for sewing up
Tweezers (optional)
Acrylic toy stuffing

## Finished size
Lizard measures 15in (38cm) long

## Tension
26 sts x 34 rows measure 4in
(10cm) square over st-st using
3.25mm needles and DK yarn
before stuffing, or needles to
give correct tension.

## Abbreviations
See page 164

## Special abbreviation
**w1** – wrap 1 stitch: take yarn between
needles to opposite side, slip one
stitch pwise from LH needle to RH
needle and take yarn back between
the needles to first side.

# How to make Lizard

**Note:** Cut a length of yarn B, 8yd (7m) long, fold in half, wind around bobbin beginning with loose ends and finishing with fold and reserve before beg.

## Body and tail

Using the long tail method and yarn A, cast on 20 sts.
**Row 1:** Purl.
**Row 2:** K2, (m1, k2) to end (29 sts).
Join on reserved bobbin of yarn B for spines and work with yarns A and B, as foll:
**Row 3:** Yarn A-p14, B-p1 with the fold of yarn, yarn A-p14.
With yarn B held double, cont in g-st carrying yarn B up WS of centre and twist yarn on WS when changing colours to avoid a hole.
**Row 4:** Yarn A-k14, yarn B-k1, yarn A-k14.
**Row 5:** Yarn A-p14, yarn B-k1, yarn A-p14.
**Row 6:** Yarn A-k6, (m1, k2) twice, k4, yarn B-k1, yarn A-k6, (m1, k2) twice, k4 (33 sts).
**Row 7:** Yarn A-p16, yarn B-k1, yarn A-p16.
**Row 8:** Yarn A-k16, yarn B-k1, yarn A-k16.
**Row 9:** As row 7.
**Rows 10 to 29:** Rep rows 8 and 9, 10 times more.
**Row 30:** Yarn A-k7, k2tog, k7, yarn B-k1, yarn A-k7, k2tog, k7 (31 sts).
**Row 31:** Yarn A-p15, yarn B-k1, yarn A-p15.
**Row 32:** Yarn A-k2tog, k13, yarn B-k1, yarn A-k13, k2tog (29 sts).
**Row 33:** Yarn A-p14, yarn B-k1, yarn A-p14.
**Row 34:** Yarn A-k14, yarn B-k1, yarn A-k14.
**Row 35:** As row 33.
**Row 36:** Yarn A-k6, k2tog, k6, yarn B-k1, yarn A-k6, k2tog, k6 (27 sts).
**Row 37:** Yarn A-p13, yarn B-k1, yarn A-p13.
Join on yarn C and work in stripes, carrying yarn loosely up side of work, as foll:

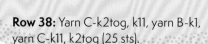

**Row 38:** Yarn C-k2tog, k11, yarn B-k1, yarn C-k11, k2tog (25 sts).
**Row 39:** Yarn C-p12, yarn B-k1, yarn C-p12.
**Row 40:** Yarn A-k12, yarn B-k1, yarn A-k12.
**Row 41:** Yarn A-p12, yarn B-k1, yarn A-p12.
**Row 42:** Yarn C-k12, yarn B-k1, yarn C-k12.
**Row 43:** Yarn C-p10, w1 (see special abbreviation), turn.
**Row 44:** Yarn C-s1k, k8, w1, turn.
**Row 45:** Yarn C-s1p, p10, yarn B-k1, yarn C-p12
**Rows 46 to 81:** Rep rows 40 to 45, 6 times more.
**Row 82:** Yarn A-k5, k2tog, k5, yarn B-k1, yarn A-k5, k2tog, k5 (23 sts).
**Row 83:** Yarn A-p11, yarn B-k1, yarn A-p11.
**Row 84:** Yarn C-k11, yarn B-k1, yarn C-k11.
**Row 85:** Yarn C-p11, yarn B-k1, yarn C-p9, w1, turn.
**Row 86:** Yarn C-s1k, k7, w1, turn.
**Row 87:** Yarn C-s1p, p to end.
**Row 88:** Yarn A-k2tog, k9, yarn B-k1, yarn A-k9, k2tog (21 sts).
**Row 89:** Yarn A-p10, yarn B-k1, yarn A-p10.
**Row 90:** Yarn C-k10, yarn B-k1, yarn C-k10.
**Row 91:** Yarn C-p10, yarn B-k1, yarn C-p8, w1, turn.
**Row 92:** Yarn C-s1k, k6, w1, turn.
**Row 93:** Yarn C-s1p, p to end.

**Row 94:** Yarn A-k4, k2tog, k4, yarn B-k1, yarn A-k4, k2tog, k4 (19 sts).
**Row 95:** Yarn A-p9, yarn B-k1, yarn A-p9.
**Row 96:** Yarn C-k9, yarn B-k1, yarn C-k9.
**Row 97:** Yarn C-p9, yarn B-k1, yarn C-p7, w1, turn.
**Row 98:** Yarn C-s1k, k5, w1, turn.
**Row 99:** Yarn C-s1p, p to end.
**Row 100:** Yarn A-k2tog, k7, yarn B-k1, yarn A-k7, k2tog (17 sts).
**Row 101:** Yarn A-p8, yarn B-k1, yarn A-p8.
**Row 102:** Yarn C-k8, yarn B-k1, yarn C-k8.
**Row 103:** Yarn C-p8, yarn B-k1, yarn C-p6, w1, turn.
**Row 104:** Yarn C-s1k, k4, w1, turn.
**Row 105:** Yarn C-s1p, p to end.
**Row 106:** Yarn A-k3, k2tog, k3, yarn B-k1, yarn A-k3, k2tog, k3 (15 sts).
**Row 107:** Yarn A-p7, yarn B-k1, yarn A-p7.
**Row 108:** Yarn C-k7, yarn B-k1, yarn C-k7.
**Row 109:** Yarn C-p7, yarn B-k1, yarn C-p5, w1, turn.
**Row 110:** Yarn C-s1k, k3, w1, turn.
**Row 111:** Yarn C-s1p, p to end.
**Row 112:** Yarn A-k7, yarn B-k1, yarn A-k7
**Row 113:** Yarn A-p7, yarn B-k1, yarn A-p7.
**Row 114:** Yarn C-k7, yarn B-k1, yarn C-k7.
**Row 115:** Yarn C-p7, yarn B-k1, yarn C-p7.
**Row 116:** Yarn A-k2tog, k5, yarn B-k1,

yarn A-k5, k2tog (13 sts).
**Row 117:** Yarn A-p6, yarn B-k1, yarn A-p6.
**Row 118:** Yarn C-k6, yarn B-k1, yarn C-k6.
**Row 119:** Yarn C-p6, yarn B-k1, yarn C-p6.
**Row 120:** Yarn A-k6, yarn B-k1, yarn A-k6.
**Row 121:** Yarn A-p6, yarn B-k1, yarn A-p6.
**Rows 122 and 123:** As rows 118 and 119.
Cont in yarn A and dec:
**Row 124:** K2tog, k9, k2tog (11 sts).
**Row 125:** Purl.
**Row 126:** K2tog, k7, k2tog (9 sts).
Break yarn and thread through sts on needle, pull tight and secure by threading yarn a second time through sts.

## Head

Using the long tail method and yarn A, cast on 20 sts.
**Row 1:** Purl.
**Row 2:** K2, (m1, k2) to end (29 sts).
**Rows 3 to 27:** Beg with a p row, work 25 rows in st-st.
**Row 28:** K1, (k2tog, k2) to end (22 sts).
**Row 29 and foll alt row:** Purl.
**Row 30:** K1, (k2tog, k1) to end (15 sts).
**Row 32:** K1, (k2tog) to end (8 sts).
Break yarn and thread through sts on needle, pull tight and secure by threading yarn a second time through sts.

## Legs (make 4)

Using the long tail method and yarn A, cast on 16 sts.
**Row 1 and foll alt row:** Purl.
**Row 2:** (K1, m1, k6, m1, k1) twice (20 sts).
**Row 4:** (K1, m1, k8, m1, k1) twice (24 sts).
**Rows 5 to 9:** Beg with a p row, work 5 rows in st-st.
**Row 10:** Cast off 6 sts, k4, m1, k2, m1, k5, cast off rem 6 sts and fasten off (14 sts).
**Row 11:** Rejoin yarn to rem sts and p to end.
**Row 12:** K1, m1, k to last st, m1, k1 (16 sts).

**Rows 13 to 15:** Beg with a p row, work 3 rows in st-st.
**Row 16:** (K2tog) to end (8 sts).
**Row 17:** Purl.
Break yarn and thread through sts on needle, pull tight and secure by threading yarn a second time through sts.

## Feet (make 4)

Using the long tail method and yarn C, cast on 8 sts.
**Row 1:** Purl.
**Row 2:** K1, (m1, k1) to end (15 sts).
**Rows 3 to 7:** Beg with a p row, work 5 rows in st-st.
**Row 8:** (K2tog, k1) to end (10 sts).
**Row 9:** Purl.
**Row 10:** (K2tog) to end (5 sts).
Break yarn and thread through sts on needle, pull tight and secure by threading yarn a second time through sts.

## Toes (make 20)

Using the long tail method and yarn C, cast on 6 sts.
**Rows 1 to 3:** Beg with a p row, work 3 rows in st-st.
**Row 4:** K1, (m1, k1) to end (11 sts).
**Rows 5 and 6:** P 1 row then k 1 row.
Break yarn and thread through sts on needle, pull tight and secure by threading yarn a second time through sts.

## Making up Lizard

**Note:** Sew up all row-end seams on right side using mattress stitch one stitch in from the edge, unless otherwise stated; a one-stitch seam allowance has been allowed for this.

### Body and tail
Sew up side edges of body and tail, beginning at tail, pushing stuffing in as you sew. This seam will be at centre of underneath.

### Head
Sew up side edges of head, stuff and sew cast-on stitches of head to cast-on stitches of body.

### Legs, feet and toes
Sew up side edges of legs from stitches pulled tight on a thread to cast-off stitches and sew up cast-off stitches. Fold cast-on stitches of legs in half and oversew, then stuff legs. Sew up side edges of feet and stuff with tweezers or tip of scissors. Sew cast-on stitches of feet to ends of legs. Sew up side edges of toes and sew five toes to each foot in a horizontal row. Sew legs to body.

### Features
Using picture as a guide, mark position of eyes with two pins and embroider eyes in black making a chain stitch for each eye, then a second chain stitch on top of first. Embroider two nostrils in black using straight stitches (see page 163 for how to begin and fasten off invisibly for the embroidery).

# Grasshopper

# Information you'll need

## Materials

Any DK (US: light worsted) yarn
(amounts given are approximate)
**Yarn A** buttermilk (10g)
**Yarn B** lime green (20g)
**Yarn C** bright green (10g)
**Yarn D** red (5g)
Oddment of black for embroidery
1 pair of 3.25mm (UK10:US3) needles
Knitters' pins and a blunt-ended needle for sewing up
Acrylic toy stuffing
10 chenille stems

## Finished size

Grasshopper measures 11in (28cm) long

## Tension

26 sts x 34 rows measure 4in (10cm) square over st-st
using 3.25mm needles and DK yarn before stuffing, or
needles to give correct tension.

## Abbreviations

See page 164

# How to make Grasshopper

## Body
Using the long tail method and yarn A, cast on 30 sts.
**Rows 1 to 3:** Beg with a p row, work 3 rows in st-st.
**Row 4:** K6, (m1, k2) 3 times, k8, (m1, k2) 3 times, k4 (36 sts).
**Rows 5 to 9:** Work 5 rows in st-st.
**Rows 10 and 11:** P 1 row, then k 1 row.
**Rows 12 to 15:** Beg with a k row, work 4 rows in st-st.
**Rows 16 to 39:** Rep rows 10 to 15, 4 times more.
**Rows 40 and 41:** P 1 row, then k 1 row.
**Rows 42 and 43:** K 1 row then p 1 row.
**Row 44:** K1, (k2tog, k3) to end (29 sts).
**Row 45:** Purl.
**Rows 46 to 49:** Rep rows 40 to 43 once.
**Row 50:** K1, (k2tog, k2) to end (22 sts).
**Row 51 and foll alt row:** Purl.
**Row 52:** K1, (k2tog, k1) to end (15 sts).
**Row 54:** K1, (k2tog) to end (8 sts).
Break yarn and thread through sts on needle, pull tight and secure by threading yarn a second time through sts.

## Neck
Using the long tail method and yarn B, cast on 30 sts and beg in rev st-st.
**Row 1:** Purl.
**Row 2:** K3, (m1, k3) to end (39 sts).
**Rows 3 to 5:** Beg with a p row, work 3 rows in rev st-st.
**Row 6:** P14, (p2tog, p1) 4 times, p13 (35 sts).
**Row 7:** Knit.
**Rows 8 to 12:** Beg with a k row, work 5 rows in rev st-st, ending with a k row.
**Row 13:** K12, (k2tog, k1) 4 times, k11 (31 sts).
**Row 14:** Purl.

**Rows 15 to 17:** Beg with a p row, work 3 rows in rev st-st, ending on a p row.
**Row 18:** (K1, k2tog) twice, k4, (k2tog, k1) 4 times, k3, (k2tog, k1) twice (23 sts).
**Row 19:** Purl.
**Row 20:** K2, (k2tog, k1) 3 times, k1, (k1, k2tog) 3 times, k2 (17 sts).
Cast off pwise.

## Head
Using the long tail method and yarn C, cast on 18 sts.
**Row 1:** Purl.
**Row 2:** K2, (m1, k2) to end (26 sts).
**Rows 3 to 11:** Beg with a p row, work 9 rows in st-st.
**Row 12:** K2tog, (k1, k2tog) to end (17 sts).
**Row 13:** Purl.
Cast off.

## Wings (make 2)
Using the long tail method and yarn B, cast on 18 sts.
**Row 1 and foll 2 alt rows:** Purl.
**Row 2:** (K1, m1, k7, m1, k1) twice (22 sts).
**Row 4:** K10, m1, k2, m1, k10 (24 sts).
**Row 6:** K11, m1, k2, m1, k11 (26 sts).
**Rows 7 to 41:** Work 35 rows in st-st.
**Row 42:** K12, k2tog, k12 (25 sts).
**Row 43 and foll 4 alt rows:** Purl.

**Row 44:** K10, k2tog, k1, k2tog, k10 (23 sts).
**Row 46:** K9, k2tog, k1, k2tog, k9 (21 sts).
**Row 48:** K8, k2tog, k1, k2tog, k8 (19 sts).
**Row 50:** K1, (k2tog, k1) to end (13 sts).
**Row 52:** K1, (k2tog, k1) to end (9 sts).
Break yarn and thread through sts on needle, pull tight and secure by threading yarn a second time through sts.

## Front legs (make 2)
Using the long tail method and yarn B, cast on 10 sts.
**Rows 1 to 25:** Beg with a p row, work 25 rows in st-st.
**Rows 26 to 41:** Change to yarn C and work 16 rows in st-st.
Break yarn and thread through sts on needle, pull tight and secure by threading yarn a second time through sts.

## Middle legs (make 2)
Using the long tail method and yarn B, cast on 10 sts.
**Rows 1 to 11:** Beg with a p row, work 11 rows in st-st.
**Rows 12 to 31:** Change to yarn C and work 20 rows in st-st.
Break yarn and thread through sts on needle, pull tight and secure by threading yarn a second time through sts.

## Back legs (make 2)

Using the long tail method and yarn B, cast on 12 sts.

**Rows 1 to 31:** Beg with a p row, work 31 rows in st-st.

Change to yarn C and dec:

**Row 32:** K2, k2tog, k4, k2tog, k2 (10 sts).

**Rows 33 to 71:** Beg with a p row, work 39 rows in st-st.

Break yarn and thread through sts on needle, pull tight and secure by threading yarn a second time through sts.

## Antennae (make 2)

Using the long tail method and yarn D, cast on 6 sts.

Beg with a p row, work in st-st until piece measures 7½in (19cm).

Break yarn and thread through sts on needle, pull tight and secure by threading yarn a second time through sts.

# Making up Grasshopper

**Note:** Sew up all row-end seams on right side using mattress stitch one stitch in from the edge, unless otherwise stated; a one-stitch seam allowance has been allowed for this.

## Body, neck and head

Sew up side edges of body and stuff. Fold cast-off stitches of neck in half and oversew. Sew up side edges of neck, stuff and sew cast-on stitches to cast on stitches of body. Fold cast-on stitches of head in half and oversew, then fold cast-off stitches in half and oversew. Stuff head and sew up row ends. Sew head to neck.

## Features

Using picture as a guide, embroider two large eyes in black on both sides of head, working an oval in chain stitch and fill it in with chain stitches. Embroider mouth using straight stitches (see page 163 for how to begin and fasten off the embroidery invisibly).

## Wings

Fold cast-on stitches of wings in half and oversew. Sew up side edges of both wings and place side by side. Sew together down middle and sew wings to back of Grasshopper.

## Front and middle legs

Place two chenille stems on wrong side of front and middle legs and sew up side edges enclosing chenille stems inside. Cut chenille stems to length of legs and gather round cast-on stitches of legs, pull tight and secure. Sew legs to body and bend legs.

## Back legs

Place two chenille stems on wrong side and sew up narrow part of legs enclosing chenille stems inside. Place another folded chenille stem at wide part at top of leg and continue sewing up wide part of legs enclosing chenille stems inside. Cut chenille stems to length of leg. Gather round cast-on stitches of legs, pull tight and secure. Sew back legs to body and bend legs.

## Antennae

Place a chenille stem on wrong side of antennae and sew up side edges. Cut chenille stem to length of antennae, sew antennae to head and curl back.

# Meerkat with Pups

# Information you'll need

## Materials
Any DK (US: light worsted) yarn
(amounts given are approximate)
**Yarn A** brown (100g) (2 separate balls needed
for intarsia)
**Yarn B** oatmeal (100g)
**Yarn C** black (5g)
**Yarn D** dark brown (10g)
Oddment of black for embroidery
1 pair of 3.25mm (UK10:US3) needles
Knitters' pins and a blunt-ended needle for sewing up
Tweezers (optional)
Acrylic toy stuffing

## Finished size
Meerkats measure 9¾in (25cm) high
Meerkat Pups measure 6¼in (16cm) high

## Tension
26 sts x 34 rows measure 4in (10cm) square over st-st
using 3.25mm needles and DK yarn before stuffing, or
needles to give correct tension.

## Abbreviations
See page 164

## Special abbreviation
**w1** – wrap 1 stitch: take yarn
between needles to opposite
side, slip one stitch pwise from
LH needle to RH needle and
take yarn back between the
needles to first side.

# How to make Meerkat

## Body
Using the long tail method and yarn A, cast on 9 sts.
**Row 1 and foll 4 alt rows:** Purl.
**Row 2:** K1, (m1, k1) to end (17 sts).
**Row 4:** K1, (m1, k2) to end (25 sts).
**Row 6:** K1, (m1, k3) to end (33 sts).
**Row 8:** K1, (m1, k4) to end (41 sts).
**Row 10:** K1, (m1, k5) to end (49 sts).
Join on yarn B and second ball of yarn A and work in intarsia in blocks of colour, twisting yarn when changing colours to avoid a hole.
**Row 11:** Yarn A-p16, yarn B-p17, yarn A (second ball)-p16.
**Row 12:** Yarn A-k16, yarn B-k1, (m1, k1) 6 times, k4, (m1, k1) 6 times, yarn A-k16 (61 sts).
**Row 13:** Yarn A-p16, yarn B-p29, yarn A-p16.
**Row 14:** Yarn A-k16, yarn B-k7, (m1, k1) 4 times, k8, (m1, k1) 4 times, k6, yarn A-k16 (69 sts).
**Row 15:** Yarn A-p16, yarn B-p37, yarn A-p16.
**Row 16:** Yarn A-k16, yarn B-k37, yarn A-k16.
**Rows 17 to 30:** Rep rows 15 and 16, 7 times more.

**Row 31:** Yarn A-p16, yarn B-p5, (p2tog) twice, p19, (p2tog) twice, p5, yarn A-p16 (65 sts).
**Row 32:** Yarn A-k16, yarn B-k1, cast off 10 sts (18 sts now on RH needle), k10, cast off 10 sts (29 sts now on RH needle), yarn A-k16 (45 sts).
Push rem sts together and cont in intarsia:
**Row 33:** Yarn A-p16, yarn B-p13, yarn A-P16.
**Row 34:** Yarn A-k16, yarn B-k13, yarn A-k16.
**Rows 35 to 45:** Rep rows 33 and 34, 5 times more, then row 33 once.
**Row 46:** Yarn A-k2, k2tog, k9, k2tog, k1, yarn B-k13, yarn A-k1, k2tog, k9, k2tog, k2 (41 sts).
**Rows 47:** Yarn A-p14, yarn B-p13, yarn A-p14.
**Row 48:** Yarn A-k14, yarn B-k13, yarn A-k14.
**Rows 49 to 53:** Rep rows 47 and 48 twice more, then row 47 once.
**Row 54:** Yarn A-k2, k2tog, k10, yarn B-k1, k2tog, k7, k2tog, k1, yarn A-k10, k2tog, k2 (37 sts).
**Row 55:** Yarn A-p13, yarn B-p11, yarn A-p13.
**Row 56:** Yarn A-k13, yarn B-k11, yarn A-k13.
**Rows 57 to 61:** Rep rows 55 and 56 twice more, then row 55 once.
**Row 62:** Yarn A-k2, k2tog, k6, k2tog, k1, yarn B-k11, yarn A-k1, k2tog, k6, k2tog, k2 (33 sts).
**Row 63:** Yarn A-p11, yarn B-p11, yarn A-p11.
**Row 64:** Yarn A-k11, yarn B-k11, yarn A-k11.
**Rows 65 to 69:** Rep rows 63 and 64 twice more, then row 63 once.
**Row 70:** Yarn A-k2, k2tog, k7, yarn B-k1, k2tog, k5, k2tog, k1, yarn A-k7, k2tog, k2 (29 sts).
**Rows 71:** Yarn A-p10, yarn B-p9, yarn A-p10.
**Row 72:** Yarn A-k10, yarn B-k9, yarn A-k10.

**Rows 73 to 75:** Rep rows 71 and 72 once, then row 71 once.
Cast off in colours as set.

## Head
Using the long tail method and yarn C, cast on 10 sts.
**Rows 1 to 3:** Beg with a p row, work 3 rows in rev st-st.
**Row 4:** Change to yarn B and p 1 row.
**Row 5:** (K1, m1) 4 times, k2, (m1, k1) 4 times (18 sts).
**Row 6:** Purl.
**Row 7:** (K1, m1) twice, k14, (m1, k1) twice (22 sts).
**Row 8:** P6, w1 (see special abbreviation), turn.
**Row 9:** S1k, k to end.
**Row 10:** Purl.
**Row 11:** K6, w1, turn.
**Row 12:** S1p, p to end.
**Row 13:** K1, m1, k to last st, m1, k1 (24 sts).
**Rows 14 to 25:** Rep rows 8 to 13 twice more (28 sts).
**Rows 26 to 28:** Work 3 rows in st-st.
**Row 29:** K3, (m1, k2) to last st, k1 (40 sts).
**Rows 30 to 42:** Work 13 rows in st-st.
**Row 43:** (K2tog, k3) to end (32 sts).
**Row 44 and foll 2 alt rows:** Purl.
**Row 45:** (K2tog, k2) to end (24 sts).
**Row 47:** (K2tog, k1) to end (16 sts).
**Row 49:** (K2tog) to end (8 sts).
Break yarn and thread through sts on needle, pull tight and secure by threading yarn a second time through sts.

## Hind legs (make 2)
Using the long tail method and yarn A, cast on 10 sts.
**Row 1:** Purl.
**Row 2:** K2, (m1, k2) to end (14 sts).
**Rows 3 to 13:** Beg with a p row, work 11 rows in st-st.
**Row 14:** K2, (m1, k2) to end (20 sts).

**Rows 15 to 19:** Work 5 rows in st-st.
**Row 20:** (K2tog, k2) to end (15 sts).
**Row 21:** Purl.
**Row 22:** (K2tog, k1) to end (10 sts).
Break yarn and thread through sts on needle, pull tight and secure by threading yarn a second time through sts.

## Forearms (make 2)

Using the long tail method and yarn B, cast on 8 sts.
**Row 1:** Purl.
**Row 2:** K1, (m1, k1) to end (15 sts).
**Rows 3 to 13:** Beg with a p row, work 11 rows in st-st.
**Row 14:** K5, w1, turn.
**Row 15:** S1p, p to end.
**Row 16:** Knit.
**Row 17:** P5, w1, turn.
**Row 18:** S1k, k to end.
**Rows 19 to 21:** Work 3 rows in st-st.
**Rows 22 to 37:** Rep rows 14 to 21 twice more.
**Row 38:** (K1, m1) twice, k1, (k2tog) twice, k1, (k2tog) twice, k1, (m1, k1) twice.
**Row 39:** Purl.
**Rows 40 to 41:** Rep rows 38 and 39 once.
**Rows 42 and 43:** Work 2 rows in st-st.
**Row 44:** (K2tog, k1) to end (10 sts).
Break yarn and thread

through sts on needle, pull tight and secure by threading yarn a second time through sts.

## Tail

Using the long tail method and yarn A, cast on 20 sts.
**Row 1:** Purl.
**Row 2:** K2tog, k to end (19 sts).
**Rows 3 to 5:** Work 3 rows in st-st.
**Rows 6 to 25:** Rep rows 2 to 5, 5 times more (14 sts).
**Row 26:** K2tog, (k2, k2tog) to end (10 sts).
**Rows 27 to 29:** Work 3 rows in st-st.
Break yarn, thread through sts on needle and leave loose.

## Eye patches (make 2)

Using the long tail method and yarn D, cast on 18 sts.
**Rows 1 and 2:** P 1 row then k 1 row.
**Row 3:** (P2tog) to end (9 sts).
Break yarn and thread through sts on needle, pull tight and secure by threading yarn a second time through sts.

## Ears (make 2)

Using the long tail method and yarn D, cast on 18 sts.
**Rows 1 to 3:** Beg with a p row, work 3 rows in st-st.
**Row 4:** K3, (k2tog) twice, k4, (k2tog) twice, k3 (14 sts).
**Row 5:** Purl.
**Row 6:** (K2tog) to end (7 sts).
Break yarn and thread through sts on needle, pull tight and secure by threading yarn a second time through sts.

## Making up Meerkat

**Note:** Sew up all row-end seams on right side using mattress stitch one stitch in from the edge, unless otherwise stated; a one-stitch seam allowance has been allowed for this.

### Body and head

Gather round cast-on stitches of body, pull tight and secure. Sew up side edges to halfway up, stuff lower body and place a ball of stuffing into sides, then sew up and stuff up to neck. Sew up side edges of nose and head leaving a gap, stuff and sew up gap. Pin and sew head to neck taking a horizontal stitch from neck, then a horizontal stitch from head and do this alternately all the way round.

### Hind legs and forearms

Sew up side edges of hind legs, stuffing as you sew. Sew across cast-on stitches then assemble hind legs on a flat surface and sew to base. Sew up side edges of forearms, stuffing as you sew. Sew arms to sides of body.

### Tail

Roll tail up from row ends to row ends beginning at shaped edge. Pull stitches on a thread tight and sew outside edge down. Sew tail to back of Meerkat.

### Eye patches and ears

Place eye patches on head and sew round outer edge. Sew up side edges of ears and with seam at centre back, sew cast-on stitches of ears to head.

### Features

Using picture as a guide, mark position of eyes with two pins and embroider eyes in black making a vertical chain stitch for each eye, then a second chain stitch on top of first (see page 163 for how to begin and fasten off invisibly for the embroidery).

## How to make Meerkat Pup

### Body

Using the long tail method and yarn A, cast on 9 sts.
**Row 1 and foll 2 alt rows:** Purl.
**Row 2:** K1, (m1, k1) to end (17 sts).
**Row 4:** K1, (m1, k2) to end (25 sts).
**Row 6:** K1, (m1, k3) to end (33 sts).
**Row 7 and foll alt row:** Purl.
**Row 8:** K12, (m1, k1) 4 times, k2, (m1, k1) 4 times, k11 (41 sts).
**Row 10:** K14, (m1, k1) 4 times, k6, (m1, k1) 4 times, k13 (49 sts).
**Rows 11 to 18:** Work 8 rows in st-st, ending on a k row.
**Row 19:** P14, (p2tog) twice, p13, (p2tog) twice, p14 (45 sts).
**Row 20:** K12, cast off 6 sts (13 sts now on RH needle), k8, cast off 6 sts (22 sts now on RH needle), k11 (33 sts).
**Rows 21 to 23:** Push rem sts tog and work 3 rows in st-st.
**Row 24:** K2, k2tog, k5, k2tog, k11, k2tog, k5, k2tog, k2 (29 sts).
**Rows 25 to 31:** Work 7 rows in st-st.
**Row 32:** K2, k2tog, k4, k2tog, k9, k2tog, k4, k2tog, k2 (25 sts).
**Rows 33 to 39:** Work 7 rows in st-st.
**Row 40:** K2, k2tog, k3, k2tog, k7, k2tog, k3, k2tog, k2 (21 sts).
**Rows 41 to 45:** Work 5 rows in st-st. Cast off.

## Head

Using the long tail method and yarn C, cast on 8 sts.

**Rows 1 and 2:** P 1 row then k 1 row.

**Rows 3 and 4:** Change to yarn B and k 1 row then p 1 row.

**Row 5:** (K1, m1) 3 times, k2 (m1, k1) 3 times (14 sts).

**Row 6:** Purl.

**Row 7:** K2, (m1, k2) to end (20 sts).

**Row 8:** P6, w1, turn.

**Row 9:** S1k, k to end.

**Row 10:** Purl.

**Row 11:** K6, w1, turn.

**Row 12:** S1p, p to end.

**Row 13:** K1, m1, k to last st, m1, k1 (22 sts).

**Rows 14 to 18:** Rep rows 8 to 12 once.

**Row 19:** K4, (m1, k2) to last 2 sts, k2 (30 sts).

**Rows 20 to 30:** Work 11 rows in st-st.

**Row 31:** (K2tog, k1) to end (20 sts).

**Row 32:** Purl.

**Row 33:** (K2tog) to end (10 sts).

Break yarn and thread through sts on needle, pull tight and secure by threading yarn a second time through sts.

## Hind legs (make 2)

Using the long tail method and yarn B, cast on 8 sts.

**Row 1:** Purl.

**Row 2:** K1, (m1, k2) to last st, m1, k1 (12 sts).

**Rows 3 to 7:** Beg with a p row, work 5 rows in st-st.

**Row 8:** K3, (m1, k3) to end (15 sts).

**Rows 9 to 13:** Work 5 rows in st-st.

**Row 14:** (K2tog, k1) to end (10 sts).

**Row 15:** (P2tog) to end (5 sts).

Break yarn and thread through sts on needle, pull tight and secure by threading yarn a second time through sts.

## Forearms (make 2)

Using the long tail method and yarn B, cast on 8 sts.

**Row 1:** Purl.

**Row 2:** K1, (m1, k2) to last st, m1, k1 (12 sts).

**Rows 3 to 11:** Beg with a p row, work 9 rows in st-st.

**Row 12:** K3, w1 (see special abbreviation), turn.

**Row 13:** S1p, p to end.

**Row 14:** Knit.

**Row 15:** P3, w1, turn.

**Row 16:** S1k, k to end.

**Row 17:** Purl.

**Rows 18 to 23:** Rep rows 12 to 17 once.

**Rows 24 and 25:** K 1 row then p 1 row.

**Row 26:** (K2tog) to end (6 sts).

Break yarn and thread through sts on needle, pull tight and secure by threading yarn a second time through sts.

## Tail

Using the long tail method and yarn A, cast on 16 sts.

**Row 1:** Purl.

**Row 2:** K2tog, k to end (15 sts).

**Rows 3 to 5:** Work 3 rows in st-st.

**Rows 6 to 21:** Rep rows 2 to 5, 4 times more (11 sts).

**Row 22:** K2tog, (k1, k2tog) to end (7 sts).

**Row 23:** Purl.

Break yarn, thread through sts on needle and leave loose.

## Eye patches (make 2)

Using the long tail method and yarn D, cast on 14 sts.

**Row 1:** Purl.

**Row 2:** (K2tog) to end (7 sts).

Break yarn and thread through sts on needle, pull tight and secure by threading yarn a second time through sts.

## Ears (make 2)

Using the long tail method and yarn D, cast on 12 sts.

**Rows 1 to 3:** Beg with a p row, work 3 rows in st-st.

**Row 4:** K2, (k2tog) 4 times, k2 (8 sts).

Break yarn and thread through sts on needle, pull tight and secure by threading yarn a second time through sts.

# Making up Meerkat Pup

**Note:** Sew up all row-end seams on right side using mattress stitch one stitch in from the edge, unless otherwise stated; a one-stitch seam allowance has been allowed for this.

## Body and head

Make up body and head, as for the adult Meerkat.

## Hind legs and forearms

Make up hind legs and forearms, as for the adult Meerkat, stuffing with tweezers or tip of scissors.

## Tail, eye patches, ears and features

Make up tail, eye patches, ears and embroider features, as for the adult Meerkat.

# Angel Fish

# Information you'll need

## Materials
Any DK (US: light worsted) yarn
(amounts given are approximate)
**Yarn A** cream (30g)
**Yarn B** black (15g)
**Yarn C** gold (5g)
Oddment of black for embroidery
1 pair of 3.25mm (UK10:US3) needles
Knitters' pins and a blunt-ended needle for sewing up
Acrylic toy stuffing
2 white chenille stems

## Finished size
Angel Fish measures 7in (18cm) across

## Tension
26 sts x 34 rows measure 4in (10cm) square over
st-st using 3.25mm needles and DK yarn before
stuffing, or needles to give correct tension.

## Abbreviations
See page 164

# How to make Angel Fish

## Head and body

Using the long tail method and yarn A, cast on 10 sts and beg in rev st-st.

**Rows 1 to 5:** Beg with a p row, work in rev st-st for 5 rows.

**Row 6:** Purl.

**Row 7:** K1, (m1, k1) to end (19 sts).

**Row 8 and foll 3 alt rows:** Purl.

**Row 9:** (K1, m1) twice, k6, (m1, k1) 4 times, k5, (m1, k1) twice (27 sts).

**Row 11:** (K1, m1) twice, k10, (m1, k1) 4 times, k9, (m1, k1) twice (35 sts).

**Row 13:** (K1, m1) twice, k14, (m1, k1) 4 times, k13, (m1, k1) twice (43 sts).

**Row 15:** (K1, m1) twice, k18, (m1, k1) 4 times, k17, (m1, k1) twice (51 sts).

Join on yarn B and C as needed and work in stripes as foll:

**Row 16:** Yarn B-purl.

**Row 17:** (K1, m1) twice, k22, (m1, k1) 4 times, k21, (m1, k1) twice (59 sts).

**Row 18:** Purl.

**Row 19:** K1, m1, k28, m1, k1, m1, k28, m1, k1 (63 sts).

**Row 20:** Yarn A-purl.

**Row 21:** K1, m1, k30, m1, k1, m1, k30, m1, k1 (67 sts).

**Row 22:** Purl.

**Row 23:** K1, m1, k32, m1, k1, m1, k32, m1, k1 (71 sts).

**Row 24:** Yarn C-purl.

**Row 25:** K1, m1, k34, m1, k1, m1, k34, m1, k1 (75 sts).

**Row 26:** Yarn B-purl.

**Row 27:** K1, m1, k36, m1, k1, m1, k36, m1, k1 (79 sts).

**Row 28 and foll alt row:** Purl.

**Row 29:** K1, m1, k77, m1, k1 (81 sts).

**Row 31:** K1, m1, k79, m1, k1 (83 sts).

**Row 32:** Yarn C-purl.

**Row 33:** K1, m1, k81, m1, k1 (85 sts).

**Rows 34 to 39:** Yarn A-work 6 rows in st-st ending with a k row.

**Rows 40 and 41:** Yarn C-p 1 row then k 1 row.

**Rows 42 to 47:** Yarn-B, work 6 rows in st-st ending with a k row.

**Row 48:** Yarn C-purl.

**Row 49:** K2tog, k38, k2tog, k1, k2tog, k38, k2tog (81 sts).

**Row 50:** Yarn A-purl.

**Row 51:** (K2tog) twice, k32, (k2tog) twice, k1, (k2tog) twice, k32, (k2tog) twice (73 sts).

**Row 52:** Purl.

**Row 53:** (K2tog) twice, k28, (k2tog) twice, k1, (k2tog) twice, k28, (k2tog) twice (65 sts).

**Row 54:** P2tog, p28, p2tog, p1, p2tog, p28, p2tog (61 sts).

**Row 55:** (K2tog) twice, k22, (k2tog) twice, k1, (k2tog) twice, k22, (k2tog) twice (53 sts).

**Row 56:** P2tog, p22, p2tog, p1, p2tog, p22, p2tog (49 sts).

**Row 57:** (K2tog) twice, k16, (k2tog) twice, k1, (k2tog) twice, k16, (k2tog) twice (41 sts).

**Row 58:** P2tog, p16, p2tog, p1, p2tog, p16, p2tog (37 sts).

**Row 59:** K2tog, k14, k2tog, k1, k2tog, k14, k2tog (33 sts).

**Row 60:** P2tog, p12, p2tog, p1, p2tog, p12, p2tog (29 sts).

**Rows 61 and 62:** K 1 row then p 1 row.

**Row 63:** (Kfb) to end (58 sts).

**Row 64:** (K1, p1) to end.

**Rows 65 and 66:** Rep row 64 twice more.

**Rows 67 to 78:** Change to yarn B and rep row 64, 12 times more.

Cast off kwise.

## Upper and lower fins (make 2)

Using the long tail method and yarn A, cast on 22 sts.

**Row 1:** Purl.

**Row 2:** K1, m1, k8, (k2tog) twice, k8, m1, k1.

**Rows 3 to 6:** Rep rows 1 and 2, twice more.

**Row 7 and all foll alt rows:** Purl.

**Row 8:** K9, (k2tog) twice, k9 (20 sts).

**Row 10:** K1, m1, k7, (k2tog) twice, k7, m1, k1.

**Row 12:** K8, (k2tog) twice, k8 (18 sts).

**Row 14:** K1, m1, k6, (k2tog) twice, k6, m1, k1.

**Row 16:** K7, (k2tog) twice, k7 (16 sts).

**Row 18:** K1, m1, k5, (k2tog) twice, k5, m1, k1.

**Row 20:** K6, (k2tog) twice, k6 (14 sts).

**Row 22:** K1, m1, k4, (k2tog) twice, k4, m1, k1.

**Row 24:** K5, (k2tog) twice, k5 (12 sts).

**Row 26:** K1, m1, k3, (k2tog) twice, k3, m1, k1.

**Row 28:** K4, (k2tog) twice, k4 (10 sts).

**Row 30:** K1, m1, k2, (k2tog) twice, k2, m1, k1.

**Row 32:** K3, (k2tog) twice, k3 (8 sts).

**Row 34:** K1, m1, k1, (k2tog) twice, k1, m1, k1.

**Row 36:** (K2tog) to end (4 sts).

Break yarn and thread through sts on needle, pull tight and secure by threading yarn a second time through sts.

## Tentacles (make 2)

Using the long tail method and yarn A, cast on 8 sts.

**Rows 1 to 29:** Beg with a p row, work 29 rows in st-st.

**Row 30:** K3, (k2tog) k3 (7 sts).

**Rows 31 to 33:** Work 3 rows in st-st.

**Row 34:** K1, (k2tog, k1) twice (5 sts). Break yarn and thread through sts on needle, pull tight and secure by threading yarn a second time through sts.

## Making up Angel Fish

**Note:** Sew up all row-end seams on right side using mattress stitch one stitch in from the edge, unless otherwise stated; a one-stitch seam allowance has been allowed for this.

### Body

Gather round cast-on stitches, pull tight and secure. Fold cast-off stitches in half and oversew. Sew up side edges of tail and stuff tail. Sew up body and head leaving a gap, stuff and sew up gap.

### Fins and tentacles

Oversew side edges of fins and stuff with tweezers or tip of scissors. Sew fins to top and bottom of Angel Fish. For tentacles, fold chenille stems in half and place fold into wrong side of stitches pulled tight and sew up side edges enclosing chenille stems inside. Cut excess chenille stems and sew tentacles to neck.

### Features

Using picture as a guide, mark position of eyes with two pins and embroider eyes in black making a vertical chain stitch for each eye, then a second chain stitch on top of first (see page 163 for how to begin and fasten off invisibly for the embroidery).

# Techniques

# Getting started

## Buying yarn

The patterns for the designs in this book are worked in double knitting (or light worsted in the US). There are many yarns on the market, from natural fibres to acrylic blends. Acrylic yarn is a good choice as it washes without shrinking, but always follow the care instructions on the ball band. Be cautious about using a brushed or mohair-type yarn if the toy is intended for a baby or a very young child, as the fibres can be swallowed.

## Safety advice

Some of the toys have small pieces and trimmings, which could present a choking hazard. Make sure that small parts are sewn down securely before giving any of the toys to a baby or young child.

## Tension

All the toys in this book are knitted on 3.25mm (UK10:US3) knitting needles. This should turn out at approximately 26 stitches and 34 rows over 4in (10cm) square. If there are less stitches, the stuffing might show through the fabric and look unsightly. If you use smaller needles the knitting will become tighter.

# Slip knot

1   Wind the yarn from the ball round your left index finger from front to back and then to front again. Slide the loop from your finger and pull the new loop through from the centre. Place this loop from back to front onto the needle that is in your right hand.

2   Pull the tail of yarn down to tighten the knot slightly and pull the yarn from the ball to form a loose knot.

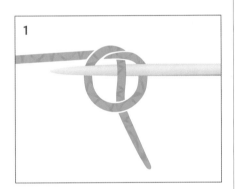

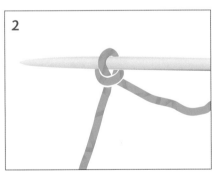

# Casting on (using the long tail method)

1   Leave a long length of yarn: as a rough guide, allow ⅜in (1cm) for each stitch to be cast on plus an extra length for sewing up. Make a slip knot.

2   Hold the needle in your right hand with your index finger on the slip knot loop to keep it in place. Wrap the loose tail end round your left thumb, from front to back. Push the needle's point through the thumb loop from front to back. Wind the ball end of the yarn round the needle from left to right.

3   Pull the loop through the thumb loop, then remove your thumb. Gently pull the new loop tight using the tail yarn.

Repeat this process until the required number of stitches are on the needle.

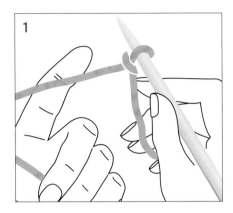

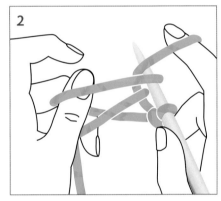

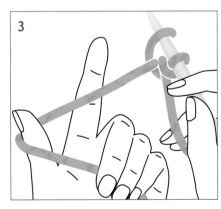

# Knitting stitches

## Knit stitch

**1** Hold needle with stitches in left hand. Hold yarn at back of work and insert point of right-hand empty needle into the front loop of the first stitch. Wrap yarn around point of right-hand needle in a clockwise direction using your index finger.

**2** With yarn still wrapped around the point, bring the right-hand needle back towards you through the loop of the first stitch. Try to keep the free yarn fairly taut but not too slack or tight.

**3** Finally, with the new stitch firmly on the right-hand needle, gently pull the old stitch to the right and off the tip of the left-hand needle. Repeat for all the knit stitches across the row.

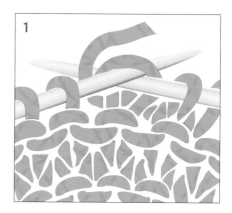

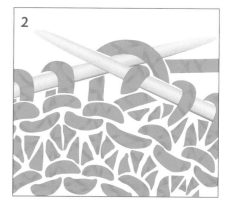

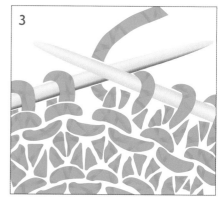

## Purl stitch

1   Hold needles with stitches in left
    hand and hold yarn at front of work.

2   Insert point of right-hand empty
    needle into the front loop of the
    first stitch. Wrap yarn around
    point of right-hand needle in an
    anticlockwise direction using index
    finger. Bring yarn back to front
    of work.

3   Now with yarn still wrapped around
    point of right-hand needle, bring it
    back through the stitch. Try to keep
    free yarn taut but not too slack or
    tight. Finally, with the new stitch
    firmly on the right-hand needle,
    gently pull the old stitch off the tip
    of the left-hand needle. Repeat for
    all the purl stitches along the row.

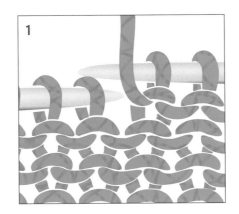

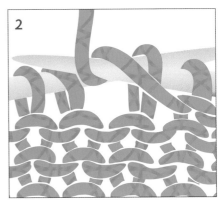

## Garter stitch (A)

This is made by knitting every row.

## Stocking stitch (B)

Probably the most commonly used stitch in knitting, this is created by knitting on the right side and purling on the wrong side.

## Reverse stocking stitch (C)

This is made in the same way as stocking stitch but the reverse side in the right side.

## Rib (D)

This is made by knitting the first stitch, then bringing the yarn between the needles to front of knitting and purling the next stitch. Take the yarn back and continue knitting then purling alternately along row. On the next row, knit all stitches that were purled on the previous row and purl all stitches that were knitted on the previous row.

## Moss stitch (E)

Knit first stitch then bring yarn forward between the needles and purl next stitch. Continue along row in this way, knitting then purling a stitch alternately. On the next row, knit each stitch that was knitted on the previous row and purl all stitches that were purled on the previous row.

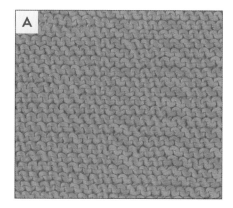
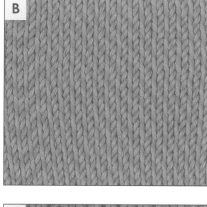
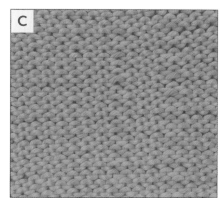
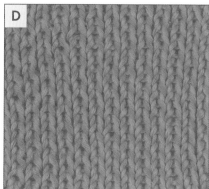
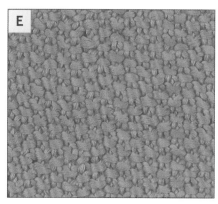

## Shaping

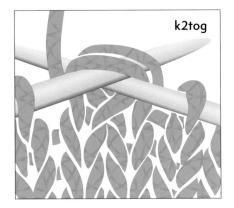

k2tog

## Decreasing

To decrease a stitch, simply knit two stitches together to make one stitch out of the two stitches, or if the instructions say k3tog, then knit three stitches together to make one out of the three stitches.

To achieve a neat appearance to your finished work, this is done as follows:

At the beginning of a knit row and throughout the row, k2tog by knitting two stitches together through the front of the loops (as shown above).

At the end of a knit row, if these are the very last two stitches in the row, then knit together through the back of the loops.

At the beginning of a purl row, if these are the very first stitches in the row, then purl together through the back of the loops. Purl two together along the rest of the row through the front of the loops.

## Increasing

Two methods are used in this book for increasing the number of stitches: m1, and kfb.

**M1** Make a stitch by picking up the horizontal loop between the needles and placing it onto the left-hand needle. Now knit into the back of it to twist it on a knit row, or purl into the back of it on a purl row.

**Kfb** Make a stitch on a knit row by knitting into the front then back of the next stitch. To do this, simply knit into the next stitch but do not slip it off. Take the point of the right-hand needle around and knit again into the back of the stitch before removing the loop from the left-hand needle. You now have made two stitches out of one.

## Knitting on stitches
### (or two-needle casting on)

1   Insert the right-hand needle from front to back between the first and second stitches on the left-hand needle and wrap the yarn around the tip of the right-hand needle from back to front.

2   Slide the right-hand needle through to the front to catch the new loop of yarn.

3   Place the new loop of yarn onto the left-hand needle, inserting the left-hand needle from front to back. Repeat this process until you have reached the required number of cast-on stitches.

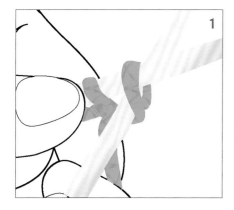

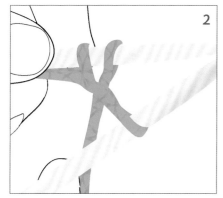

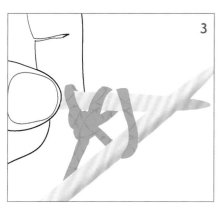

## Intarsia

Blocks of colour are worked using the intarsia technique. Twist the two different yarns together at the back of the work with each colour change to prevent holes appearing. Once finished, weave in ends at the back of the work.

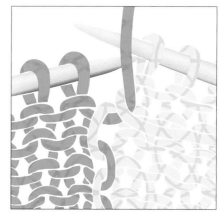

## Casting off

1   Knit two stitches onto the right-hand needle, then slip the first stitch over the second and let it drop off the needle. One stitch remains on the needle.

2   Knit another stitch so you have two stitches on the right-hand needle again.

Repeat the process until only one stitch is left on the left-hand needle. Break the yarn, thread it through the remaining stitch and pull tight to fasten off.

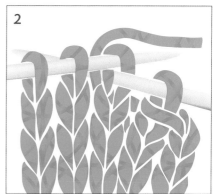

## Making-up instructions

### Mattress stitch (A)

Join row ends by taking small straight stitches back and forth on the right side of work, one stitch from the edge.

### Over-sewing (B)

Pieces can also be joined by over-sewing on the wrong side and turning the piece right side out. For smaller pieces or pieces that cannot be turned, oversew on the right side.

### Backstitch (C)

Bring needle out at the beginning of the stitch line, make a small stitch and bring the needle out slightly further along the stitch line. Insert the needle at the end of the first stitch and bring it out still further along the stitch line. Continue in the same way to create a line of joined stitches.

### Stuffing and aftercare

Spend a little time stuffing your knitted toy evenly. Acrylic toy stuffing is ideal for this; make sure to use plenty, but not so much that it stretches the knitted fabric so the stuffing can be seen through the stitches. Tweezers are useful for stuffing small parts.

Washable filling is recommended for all the stuffed toys so that you can hand-wash them with a non-biological

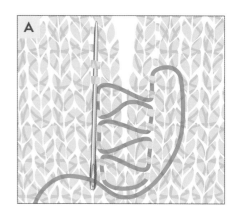

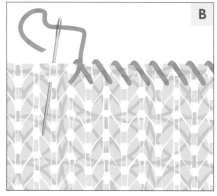

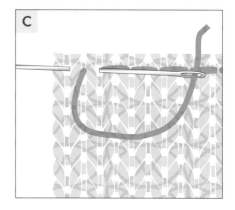

detergent. Do not spin or tumble dry, but gently squeeze the excess water out, arrange the toy into its original shape, and leave it to dry.

## Special instructions

### Threading yarn through stitches

Sometimes the instructions will tell you to 'thread yarn through stitches on needle, pull tight and secure'. To do this, first break the yarn, leaving a long end, and thread a blunt-ended sewing needle with this end. Pass the needle through all the stitches on the knitting needle, slipping each stitch off the knitting needle in turn. Draw the yarn through the stitches. To secure, pass the needle once again through all the stitches in a complete circle and pull tight.

# Finishing touches

## Embroidery

To begin embroidery invisibly, tie a knot in the end of the yarn. Take a large stitch through the work, coming up to begin the embroidery. Allow the knot to disappear through the knitting and be caught in the stuffing. To fasten off invisibly, sew a few stitches back and forth through the work, inserting the needle where the yarn comes out.

## Chain stitch (D)

Bring the needle up through your work to start the first stitch and hold down the thread with the left thumb. Now insert the needle in the same place and bring the point out a short distance away. Keeping the working thread under the needle point, pull the loop of thread to form a chain.

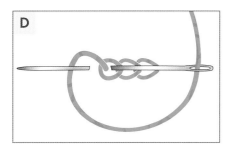

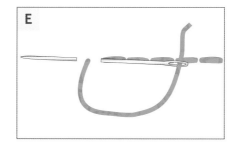

## Backstitch (E)

Bring needle out at the beginning of the stitch line, make a small stitch and bring the needle out slightly further along the stitch line. Insert the needle at the end of the first stitch and bring it out still further along the stitch line. Continue in the same way to create a line of joined stitches.

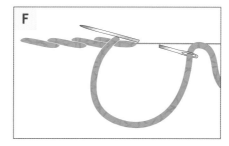

## Stem stitch (F)

Starting at the left-hand side and working towards the right-hand side, work small stitches backwards along the stitch line with the thread always emerging on the same side of the previous stitch.

## Straight stitch

Come up to start the embroidery at one end of the stitch then go back down at the end of the stitch, coming up in a different place to start the next stitch.

## Satin stitch

Work a series of straight stitches closely together.

## Twisted cord

1   Cut even strands of yarn to the number and length stated in the pattern and knot each end. Anchor one end: you could tie it to a door handle or chair, or ask a friend to hold it for you.

2   Take the other end and twist until it is tightly wound.

3   Hold the centre of the cord, and place the two ends together. Release the centre, so the two halves twist together. Smooth it out and knot the ends together.

# Abbreviations

**alt**    alternate

**approx**    approximately

**beg**    beginning

**cm**    centimetre(s)

**cont**    continue

**dec**    decrease/decreasing

**DK**    double knitting

**foll**    following

**g-st**    garter stitch: knit every row

**g**    gram(s)

**inc**    increase/increasing

**k**    knit/knitting

**k2tog or k3tog**    knit two or three stitches together: if these are the very last in the row, then work through back of loops

**kfb**    make two stitches out of one: knit into the front then the back of the next stitch

**kwise**    knitwise

**LH**    left hand

**m1**    make one stitch: pick up horizontal loop between the needles and work into the back of it to twist it

**mm**    millimetre(s)

**patt**    pattern

**p**    purl

**p2tog or p3tog**    purl two or three stitches together: if these stitches are the very first in the row, then work together through back of loops

**pwise**    purlwise

**rem**    remaining

**rep**    repeat(ed)

**rev st-st**    reverse stocking stitch: purl on the right side, knit on the wrong side

**RH**    right hand

**RS**    right side

**s1k**    slip one stitch knitways

**s1p**    slip one stitch purlways

**st(s)**    stitch(es)

**st-st**    stocking stitch: knit on the right side, purl on the wrong side

**tbl**    through back of loop(s)

**tog**    together

**WS**    wrong side

**yf**    yarn forward

**( )**    repeat instructions between brackets as many times as instructed

**\***    repeat from * as instructed

**\*\*or\*\*\***    repeat between asterisks

# Conversions

## Knitting needles

| UK | Metric | US |
|---|---|---|
| 14 | 2mm | 0 |
| 13 | 2.25mm | 1 |
| 12 | 2.75mm | 2 |
| 11 | 3mm | – |
| 10 | 3.25mm | 3 |
| – | 3.5mm | 4 |
| 9 | 3.75mm | 5 |
| 8 | 4mm | 6 |
| 7 | 4.5mm | 7 |
| 6 | 5mm | 8 |
| 5 | 5.5mm | 9 |
| 4 | 6mm | 10 |
| 3 | 6.5mm | 10.5 |
| 2 | 7mm | 10.5 |
| 1 | 7.5mm | 11 |
| 0 | 8mm | 13 |
| 000 | 10mm | 15 |

## Yarn weight

| UK | US |
|---|---|
| Double knitting | Light worsted |

## Terminology

| UK | US |
|---|---|
| Cast off | Bind off |
| Stocking stitch | Stockinette stitch |
| Tension | Gauge |
| Yarn round needle | Yarn over |
| Moss stitch | Seed stitch |

First published 2022 by
Guild of Master Craftsman Publications Ltd, Castle Place, 166 High Street, Lewes,
East Sussex BN7 1XU

Text © Sarah Keen, 2022
Copyright in the Work © GMC Publications Ltd, 2022

Reprinted 2024

ISBN 978-1-78494-616-6

Publisher  Jonathan Bailey
Production  Jim Bulley
Senior Project Editor  Virginia Brehaut
Pattern Checker  Jude Roust
Design Manager  Robin Shields
Designer  Lynne Lanning
Photographer  Andrew Perris
Illustrator  Rhiann Bull

Colour origination by GMC Reprographics
Printed and bound in China

## Acknowledgements

Special thanks to the manager, Cynthia, of Clare Wools Aberystwyth, for her wonderful shop and all her wonderful wool, www.clarewools.co.uk; for the scores of yarns stocked, and her assistance in selecting only the best for each design to complete this book. And, of course, her squeal of delight on seeing each new design knitted up!

Also, thanks to family and friends for their enthusiasm and enjoyment of the designs as they were completed.

And a huge thanks to all the team at GMC for making this book possible.

## Dedicated to

Cynthia and Helen,
from my local
Wool Shop.

# Index

To order a book, contact:
GMC Publications Ltd
Castle Place, 166 High Street,
Lewes, East Sussex,
BN7 1XU
United Kingdom
Tel: +44 (0)1273 488005
www.gmcbooks.com